2.91
Xuân Tân Mùi
Anh chị Bình, Dang

The
Etheric Body
of Man

QUEST BOOKS
are published by
The Theosophical Society in America,
Wheaton, Illinois 60189-0270,
a branch of a world organization
dedicated to the promotion of the unity of
humanity and the encouragement of the study of
religion, philosophy, and science, to the end that
we may better understand ourselves and our place in
the universe. The Society stands for complete
freedom of individual search and belief.
In the Classics Series well-known
theosophical works are made
available in popular editions.
For more information
write or call.
1-312-668-1571

Cover art by Jane Evans

The Etheric Body of Man

The Bridge of Consciousness

Formerly published under the title *Man Incarnate*

Lawrence J. Bendit
and Phoebe D. Bendit

*This publication made possible with
the assistance of the Kern Foundation*

The Theosophical Publishing House
Wheaton, Ill. U.S.A.
Madras, India/London, England

Published by the Theosophical Publishing House, a depart-
ment of the Theosophical Society in America.

Library of Congress Cataloging in Publication Data
Bendit, Phoebe Daphne Payne, 1891-
    The etheric body of man.

    (A Quest book)
    First published in 1957 under title: Man incarnate.
    1. Aura.   2. Astral projection.   I. Bendit
Laurence, John, 1898-   joint author.   II. Title
ISBN: 0-8356-0489-6   BP573.A8B46   1977 133.9 76-46930

Printed in the United States of America

CONTENTS

INTRODUCTION

One of the most important revolutions in human history was the replacement of religious and philosophical authority by experiment. In Western culture the Greek philosophical methods and ideas held sway over the minds of men and women for centuries. Deduction, not experiment, determined what was believed about the natural world and its processes. The Roman Catholic Church absorbed many of the early Greek ideas, especially those of Aristotle, into its theology. In its turn, this theology determined both what was commonly believed and what was permitted to be believed about the universe. The curious notion of testing theory by experiment had not yet taken root. It is little wonder that humanity's technologies advanced slowly in these times.

Galileo was among the first to actively pursue knowledge through experiment; or at the very least, he was the first of the experimenters to widely publicize his methods and findings. His curiousity and his genius for experiment were both great, and not unexpectedly he soon discovered that the workings of the world and universe were not what the Greeks had "deduced" them to be. Since the Greek theories were now largely Church dogma, and since Galileo realized they were wrong and said so, tremendous conflict arose. He was forced to recant and placed under arrest by the Church. He continued to experiment but was forbidden to publish his findings. The experimental method, the basis of all science, eventually won out, but only after much suffering and struggle. The inertia of the Church's theology, being great, has carried its theories through even to this day; they are still studied, copied and accepted, though they often fail if put to the test of experiment. Thus it is generally accepted that in matters of physical reality, of natural processes and the like, it is science, and its experimental method, which is to be relied upon, and not the thoughtful nor fanciful deductions of theologians and philosophers. If a theory is so constructed that it cannot be tested, science has nothing to say about it one way or the other (though individual scientists may); philosophy may

spin its webs of causation behind causation behind causation, but science makes tools, saves lives, and prints this book.

This dialectic could be argued more extensively and certainly persuasively, but the scientific method itself is now beginning to strip the validity from this division of science and religion.

It is definitely true that much philosophical, metaphysical and religious speculation is no more than tall yarns dressed in choice words, but a certain fraction of this "speculation", not arrived at through experimental means, may yet prove to have a foundation in reality. The experimental road to knowledge may not be the only one available. The evidence for this turns up in a simple comparison of present-day experimentally-based physical theory and certain metaphysically grown concepts rooted in perceptual capacities beyond the five senses.

It is no great effort, of course, to draw similarities between any collections of ideas, and we must avoid the fool's road of oversimplification and the ignoring of contradictory results. The study, made rigorously, will finally show whether the processes described by psychic means are genuine or fanciful. It is better for all concerned that the truth—whatever it is—be found out.

Science and religion were once inseparable; magic was the realm of the priest/scientist, and whether manipulating occult forces or flint and tinder to make fire, it was the same individual who performed the ritual, and it was all magical to the uninitiated. As religion became more rigid, the separation between science and theology widened; experiment took hold as an idea, and before long what was discovered to be true came to arms with what the Church pronounced to be true. The experimenters, like Galileo, suffered. It is probably much in reaction to this suffering that science still shies from anything which smacks of religion or metaphysics.

Why then is the tide beginning to turn? Why is there now at least a ripple, if not a flood, of interest within the scientific community for metaphysical descriptions of reality?

The reason is historical: as a result (largely of the elegant

theories of Newton describing the motions of objects, planets, the force of gravity, the reflections and refractions of light, the manipulations of numbers through calculus, and other equally profound insights into the operations of the familiar universe), a school of thought arose which saw the universe as a complicated but well-defined machine, faithfully following with infinite precision the laws which Newton so clearly expressed. This school of Materialism prospered and grew with every advance of science until the late nineteenth century. Instruments, ever more precise, discovered that the universe was not; Newton's laws were only *approximately* true. The universe, so recently thought to be easily understood and really quite simple, suddenly grew very strange. As science has advanced in the last century, this strangeness has only increased. "Strangeness" has even become a label for a certain property of subatomic particles. Today we are aware of being subject to different laws. One of the foremost of these is the Uncertainty Principle, which in one sense states in a formal, mathematical way, the scientific realization that the observer *always* influences and changes the observed. Scientifically speaking, there is no such thing as objectivity. The universe and its inhabitants are inextricably bound into a whole; everything is connected.

To more and more good scientists these discoveries summon forth an eerie presence from the subconscious. This is not new ground we are breaking, but ancient ground, rich with the works of generations of religious minds, covered by unspoken mysteries, glinting here and there with traces of long-forgotten truths.

Centuries ago, the scientist set out on a quest for truth, taking no one's word for what was real, dedicated only to experiment and discovery. Surely with such freedom, objective reality could be found. But it was not to be, for the world was not apart from its curious experimenters, and now, having trod carefully on a well-chosen road to truth, we find ourselves rejoining another road, another way to truth from which we had separated many years past.

Is such supposition meaningful? Are we really at a rejoin-

ing of paths, or merely caught in a fiction of semantic origins? The way to find out, of course, is to experiment. Experiments in quantum mechanics, particle physics, and the like have suggested these relationships which interest us, but only tangentially, as a by-product. We need experiments devoted specifically to the task of investigating certain metaphysically and religiously derived ideas whose validity has been suggested by other experiments.

Clairvoyants speak of auras and channels of energy within and outside of the body; others speak of out-of-the-body experiences; some claim life extends beyond physical death. Unfortunately, today's instruments are not sensitive to these events. This is sufficient evidence for many to dismiss such claims as fantasy, but others point back by way of example to the time—most of human history—when no instruments existed which were sensitive to radio frequencies, yet we know now that the stars were emitting them despite our ignorance. It is not unreasonable to desire to discover whether some of the reports of clairvoyants have a basis in fact.

Phoebe Payne Bendit, one of the authors of The Etheric Body of Man, was a clairvoyant, trained and considered highly skilled in what some might consider an ability of questionable substance. Laurence Bendit, the co-author, took his M.D. from Cambridge and specialized in psychiatry. The two met, collaborated, and finally married. The partnership was most productive and beneficial. Their marriage was analogous to that which may yet come about between science and religion. Here was a well-trained and original man of science, and with him a woman equally well-trained and original in her own specialty, one quite unlike that of her mate. Between them they wrote a number of carefully researched, well-written and informative books. What is so compelling about their works, the present one included, is the caution, the detail, and the rigorousness of their reporting. These two were very clearly not dreamers, nor fools, nor self-deluded seekers after a "greater reality". They were very conscious of the demands of the scientific method; there was nothing sloppy about their work; and there were no beliefs

expressed which carried the common undercurrent of an emotional need to believe. These two were bright, and careful, and knew what they were about.

As we are just now seeing developing in the scientific community a willingness to investigate such things as auras, energy fields within the body, and other ideas once excluded from scientific scrutiny and experiment, we now lack the necessarily acceptable techniques and instruments to test the claims which are made. These techniques and instruments are being developed, but the literature of the field was largely authored in days past. In many ways the study resembles astronomy, which up until the late 1950's was a purely non-experimental, observational science. For centuries all we could do was listen to the reports of reliable observers. We naturally gave most credence to those astronomers who reported carefully and in detail their observations. With time and training and patience and a telescope we might duplicate those observations, but it has only been since the beginning of the space age that we've been able to experiment in space, rather than just look at it. or than read the reports of those who do.

Being in essentially the same straits with clairvoyant reports and metaphysical theories, we would seem most wisely guided by paying heed to what the most responsible of these authors have to say in their studies, and from these reports see if we can't develop experiments to test for validity. That we can do little more at the moment than muddle around is no more discrediting than the fact that we can't begin to journey to even the nearest neighboring star. Metaphysics, exobiology and astrophysics are simply difficult fields in which to experiment, and in them a great deal of hard work and long hours are ahead.

The reporting in this book may someday prove to be erroneous in full or in part, or it may prove to be an accurate piece to the larger puzzle. In any event, we do not today have significant experimental evidence one way or the other, and we must therefore be guided by what evidence exists, and that is wholly internal. This evidence is excellent: the work was

done by two responsible and clearly level-headed individuals who were not scientifically unsophisticated; their rigor recalls that of Tycho Brahe, who catalogued the stars and planets so precisely that a young associate, Johannes Kepler, was able from these observations to derive three fundamental laws of planetary motion. Kepler, a clergyman, included along with these brilliant deductions any number of spurious and fanciful notions about magic numbers, and it is important to note that this same tendency is surely to be found in the metaphysical world as well. No field is without its healthy quota of kooks of every stripe and degree; but just as this does not deter science elsewhere, it rightly should not deter it here. The metaphysical world will benefit from its partnership with science, for science will flush from their haven all those whose wild claims had previously gone without serious challenge, seemingly safe from testing or contradiction.

A serious study of the metaphysical literature will reveal much that is non-trivial; what is necessary now is to seek out the best of what has gone before: story, experiment, observation and theory, and from it develop a conscientious program of experiment.

The Etheric Body of Man is not a survey of the clairvoyant reality, but rather a study of a small area within the larger realm of human existence. This study confines itself primarily to what is termed the Vital Etheric Field, one of several interpenetrating fields which are said to compose the human body. As it is considered the densest of these increasingly rarefied fields, it is the best candidate for study. This book should serve us well in preparing for such an investigation; it is one of the clearest and least presupposing guides yet available.

George Koch
Mill Valley, Calif.
1976

Preface

When we set out to write this small book we hoped to be able to do so in such a form that it would be easily intelligible to the general public. But as we went on it became evident that without taking into account both empirical observation, matters of medical and psychological knowledge and principles derived from ancient occult sources, it would be impossible to do more than give a superficial notion of the subject. And this, we saw, would be both as dangerous and as inadequate as popular medicine, where a little knowledge even of real facts, but divorced from its deeper context, can do more harm than good.

Moreover, the more we studied the matter of man incarnate from the viewpoint of spiritual philosophy, the more profound became the subject. For it appeared ever clearer that man on earth, in a dense body, is in a sense as completely spiritual as in any after-life or at any stage between lives. His body is, in effect, Spirit seen and experienced in terms of space-time. Without the body, man as naked Spirit would be left in a subjective state, with no consciousness, and hence no possibility of gaining objective experience or realizing himself for what he is.

It is axiomatic in spiritual science that progress and achievement have to take place while in an earthly body. Indian philosophy, Hindu or Buddhist, teaches this—and it is implicit in the Catholic Christian Church—that a saint has to have been proved to be so by actions performed in the material world before his death.

It follows that if one really and completely understood the mystery of human incarnation, one would understand the whole problem of the nature of man, and, indeed, of life itself.

It is perhaps unfortunate that here and there specialized terms have had to be used, particularly some derived from Sanskrit. But this is where no adequate English words will exactly express what one wants to say.

Needless to say, much that is said here is quite unscientific, taking this word in its popular sense, not in the broader one of "knowledge-making". Yet as one studies questions such as these it is surprising how much light tradition or empiricism can shed on scientific knowledge, and vice versa: each supplies a certain lack in the other, and leads to a stereoscopic view of the subject, so that understanding is the richer. But as both science and understanding are always progressive, it follows that this view must also change. It is indeed one of the troubles of writing a book such as this, that the writers are apt to feel that by the time it is in print it is already out of date. Nevertheless, if the basis be sound it serves as a stepping-stone on the road to further study: not towards any goal, because in the life of the mind whenever one reaches a certain goal one finds that it is not a goal but a sign-post pointing the way to a further stage of understanding.

Yet when all is said and done, it is one of the joys of such study that there is always more to discover. Life is never dull, whatever one's age, when the road is open before one and seems to run on indefinitely so long as space and time endure.

L. J. Bendit

I feel strongly that in a study of this kind it is necessary to say what I personally mean by clairvoyance. There is much misunderstanding attached to extrasensory perception which is, after all, merely a means and not an end.

In the physical world one can learn much by observation, but it does not at all follow that what is observed is understood. In using the faculty of clairvoyance one still uses external observation, and sees much that is not necessarily deciphered accurately. All such vision is personal, and not to

be confused with spiritual illumination. The evidence of the physical senses can never be accepted as proof of ultimate reality. Neither can that of the psychic sense, for the latter, like the former, is a useful servant but a dangerous guide.

All extra-sensory perception has to pass through the mind of the percipient and is therefore biased by its mental images, intellectual interests, and the neutral tone and coloring of that mind. To me the most legitimate use of my capacity is to make such observations as I can, and present these for acceptance or rejection in precisely the same way as we present the other ideas in this study. At best they perhaps serve as illustrations of the many subtle things we have tried to convey, at worst they can be regarded as fantasies and thus dismissed. But after thirty years of observation of the human etheric field in diagnostic work for both physical and psychological cases, I can at least state simply that clairvoyant observation has been useful and acceptable.

Phoebe D. Bendit
Camberley, 1957.

1

The Aura

Some thirty-five years ago a book appeared which, for the first time in scientific history, described an aura which was said to exist around the body of living creatures, which was invisible to ordinary vision, and which varied in states of health or disease. Moreover, it told how, by the use of certain chemical screens, this aura could be brought within the range of sight of any ordinary person. This book, *The Human Atmosphere,* was by a physician of consultant rank, W. J. Kilner, M.A., M.B., Ch.B., M.R.C.P., who had been on the staff of St. Thomas's Hospital, London, and was published by a most reputable firm.* Hence it was of a nature which meant that it was no mere cranky document, but represented a piece of serious research. What might have followed, had Kilner lived, it is difficult to say. In those days phenomena of extra-sensory perception were still being cried down as pure illusion, if not fraud, and it seems as if the same fate might have befallen Kilner like other pioneers, that he would have been dubbed a crank who had "gone off the rails", chasing some hobby of his own imagination. Yet what he had done was simply to proclaim, from a scientific angle, a thing which has always been familiar to people of even small degree of clair-voyance, or other forms of psychic sensitivity.

What it amounts to is that the skin is not the outmost extension in space of the human being except as regards his dense physique. Outside it there is a region of emanations which though subtle and beyond the range of normal vision, or even of the most sensitive photographic film, is neverthe-less intimately connected with the body and its functions

---

*Kegan Paul, Trench, Trubner & Co., London, and E. P. Dutton, New York, 1920.

while alive. After death it is no longer there. It may be argued at this point that one is dealing with so mundane a thing as the heat radiated from the living body, so that when the coldness of death sets in it has vanished; and indeed it may be that some part of the aura described by Kilner is associated with heat. But that would leave unanswered why a piece of hot metal does not have precisely the same aura as a living body, visible to the eye with the help of Kilner's dicyanin screens.* Moreover, it would not tell why the contours of this aura altered in the particular way which Kilner describes where there is no measurable change in local or general body temperatures.

In the light of modern research it can be further suggested that what is being made visible is simply an electromagnetic field such as is created by all physiological action, even if it is in the nature of minute potentials of a few microvolts. This is certainly nearer the mark, since these potential differences appear to be directly related to events taking place in mind and body, in other words, to vital phenomena.

Again, many people in the last decades have found themselves able, by using apparatus varying from supposedly electrical machines costing a great deal to simple divining rods or pendulums or even the bare hand, to diagnose the seat of disease and the state of health and vitality of patients. It seems reasonable to think that by these means they too are concerned with the field of emanations around the body and, for that matter, within it. That they sometimes say that they have measured wave-lengths or rates of vibration corresponding to different organs and different states of health is quite unproved from a scientific angle. But it is not untenable that they may have been able to detect alterations from a certain norm in an energy field which is directly linked with the dense body, even if the supposed "rates" are only symbols and not actual measurements.

---

*The exact description of these screens is not given. They consisted of glass cells containing an alcoholic solution of a coal-tar dye, dicyanin, the chemical composition of which is not stated.

All these facts put together only go to confirm what clair-voyance has to say about the matter. And while no two clairvoyants probably agree exactly as to details, there is a very great measure of agreement among them; first that such an aura or atmosphere as Kilner describes actually exists; secondly that it presents a projected picture of the physical vital, and of the psycho-spiritual state of the person to whom it belongs.

In this book, which is the result of trying to set down the findings of empirical observation and study, much will be said which, from the angle of science, is pure hypothesis. It is the result largely of one person's clairvoyant investigations, linked to medical psychological knowledge, and to principles derived from other sources, many of them traditional and very ancient. Hence, no authority is claimed, since clair-voyance is so individual a matter, and, moreover, its range varies so greatly not only according to the type of the indi-vidual, but to the degree to which he is trained. There are many people who are to some extent clairvoyant and who are able to *see* for themselves something of the things of which we shall write but few of them, unfortunately, have an inquiring and critical mind, and this militates against objectivity and clarity of perception. On the other hand, continual self-criticism and self-examination, as well as constant effort and repeated experiment, far from detracting from one's powers, increase them and extend both their range and their sharp-ness of focus. Yet even so, as inner awareness grows, though the things seen remain the same, they are ever seen differ-ently and with new meaning. All that this book can do is to be suggestive, in the hope that it may stimulate the reader to consider his own experience and intuition so that he can assess for himself something of the deeper truths about human life in a dense and semi-dense body.

The aura around living beings, seen clairvoyantly, is far larger than the restricted *atmosphere* by Kilner. His techni-que appears to have made visible only the inner layers of the whole, that part which roughly follows the outline of the body. Subtler methods of observation show that the total

energy field extends a considerable way beyond, and that the general form is ovoid. In a normal person who is alert and active, it would be roughly two yards across at its widest point, while it would extend roughly two feet above the head and below the feet. But these dimensions are very variable, far more so than those of the denser inner aura round the body.

The larger, ovoid aura is an elaborate structure of lines of force which indicate both the actual processes of thought and feeling from moment to moment and the potentialities, developed and undeveloped, of the spiritual and psychic aspects of the individual. It is, in short, a mirror in which the whole man is reflected at every stage of his personal development.

A particular feature of the aura which stands out to the vision of every competent clairvoyant is a series of quickly moving vortices of energy situated at certain points of the body. These were known of old, and are often found represented in ancient diagrams, whether of East or West, on statues or carvings, and so on. Sometimes—as in the halo of Christian saints, or in the caste-marks of Hindus—a particular one of these centers is emphasized and the rest left out. But in any case they appear pretty constantly both in ancient traditions and in the perceptions of modern sensitives. Moreover, it is not by any means essential to be able to *see* to realize their existence, and many people become aware of them through their hands when examining a person with an extra-sensory touch.

Kilner does not appear to have gone far enough in his researches to have touched on this aspect of the aura, but some knowledge of it inevitably comes with any deeper investigation which may be done, by whatever means. Moreover, these centers are a most important feature of the aura in that they extend right through both the inner and the ovoid aura, and are connecting links between the two. Their Sanskrit name, *chakra,* is the word for a wheel, and is very suitable and descriptive. They are organs of the psychic aspect of every living creature, and highly complex in structure. Moreover, they are intimately linked with the controlling

mechanism of the dense body through the nervous system and the endocrine glands. At this point, where we are dealing only with the visible aspects of the aura, we will say no more. But some idea of them will be given in the next chapter.

2

The Vital Field

The common description of the vital field (for which other current names are the "health aura" or "etheric body") is as a silvery haze extending a few inches beyond the skin. Many people can see something of this fairly easily under special conditions. Some find Kilner's dicyanin screens are useful. Many more can use ultra-violet light. Others acquire a knack of using their eyes, unfocused, in a half-light so that the outer parts of the retina come into play, while some use straight clairvoyance. For the most part the impression is of a vague, undifferentiated field. Slightly more definite vision shows what appears to be a rather dark and static layer about half an inch deep, near the skin, beyond which extends a more luminous and apparently active band. A detail often noted is of streamers coming from the tips of the fingers.* To see the intricate structural detail of the field, however, requires much finer focus.

Actually, to speak of the aura as outside the body is misleading. In reality it penetrates every particle of the body as well as extending beyond it. Indeed, the body can be looked upon as a consolidation of dense matter inside the auric field. It is not far from true to say that the etheric or vital aura is the matrix in which the body grows, just as the embryo does in the womb; but this womb is not hollow; it is filled with the energy counterparts of every organ, every cell, every cell-nucleus, molecule, chemical atom and subdivision of these atoms, in a series of energy levels. Thus, if we consider the

---

* Some recent experiments with Kirlian photography also show light streamers though there is disagreement among scientists as to exactly what these are—whether they are aural emanations or some other energy force.

physical body alone, seen etherically, it consists of a structure· of lines of force or energy patterns more or less fixed, anchored to the physical matter of the tissues. The converse is also true, that the tissues exist as such only because of the vital field behind them.

It is difficult to find exact language in which to describe things invisible to normal sense perception. Yet to describe these extra-sensory perceptions, ordinary language must be used, even if this is only partly adequate. Hence what is said below must be taken as only relatively true, and suggestive rather than strictly factual.

The grey mist, carefully examined, is in reality no more grey than a pearl. Like a pearl, it is suffused with color, but unlike it the color is constantly moving and shimmering. The nearest analogy is the aurora borealis where, against a luminous background, one sees occasional flushes of delicate rose or green, trembling and shimmering, and sometimes giving an impression of waves like wind over a cornfield. This is quite different from the coloring of the outer, ovoid area, where the hues are stronger and more brilliant, reminding one of a rapidly changing sunset. One of the reasons for this is that the *matter* of which the outer aura consists is less dense than that of the inner, as the atmosphere is less dense than the sea and the earth inside it.

In the older theosophical literature it is suggested that there are different layers of auras, interpenetrating one another, and to all intents and purposes functionally independent. We are thus told of an aura which represents the *mental body* where thought takes place, an *astral body* for feeling processes, and an *etheric* or *vital body* associated with the dense physical body. In these days, when differentiations between energy and matter are fading, and functions are being increasingly thought of as integrated parts of a whole, it appears more useful to consider the whole aura as one. In the body, skeleton, muscles, nerves, viscera, etc., are seen as one organism and not as a collection of separate tissues. Moreover, the interlocking of psychological and physiological states is not known to be so close that however one may be

able to analyze out thought as distinct from feeling, and both from biochemical phenomena, it is evident that the outer, or psychological, and the inner, or physiological, layers of the aura are intrinsically part of a single structure.

In this study, however, we shall be concerned principally with the inner or health, aura, more aptly known as the vital or etheric field: that aspect of man which is in direct relationship with the dense physical body, and through which all psychological phenomena associated with physical consciousness have to play. This vital aura is, in effect, the bridge mechanism between the objective physical world and individual within. No subjective experience can reach the physical brain without it, no impact from the outer world can reach the mind except by means of it. If it is paralyzed or broken by drug, injury or death, physical unconsciousness results.

Occult science teaches that the energies involved in vital phenomena are in nature the same as those of the remainder of the electromagnetic range. They are subtler and have a shorter wave length, while potential differences are very much smaller. Something of this is gradually being recognized in the scientific field, where it is found that there are consistent differences of the order of some microvolts between parts of living organism.[1] Here, however, we are dealing with energies still finer: possibly expressible in terms of micro-microvolts (one billionth of a volt) rather than microvolts (or millionths).

It is not surprising to find that the aura, being electromagnetic, is made up of fields of energy at right angles to one another—just as an electrical field is always at right angles to its related magnetic field. In the human being three main currents of energy have been observed.

First there is one which is vertical, running up and down the central axis of the body, corresponding to the spine. This is similar to alternating electric current, entering the system

---

[1] H. S. Burr, "Field Theory in Biology" in *The Scientific Monthly,* Vol. LXIV, No. 3, March 1947, Yale University School of Medicine.

at the head and at the opposite end of the spine. This primary current, said to run "between sun and earth", "from heaven above, from earth below", induces other currents at right angles to itself which flow between the spine and the outer edge of the aura. These are the radiations described by reliable observers. These in turn induce yet other currents, also at right angles, which flow like a constant stream round and round the auric field.

We thus have a vital aura consisting of an interweaving mesh of streams of energy, like a three dimensional basketwork, with the spinal current as an axis. This axis holds the aura together and gives it coherent form. The whole can be compared to a magnet surrounded by lines of force, in which metal filings are drawn into a pattern in the magnetic field. It can be tentatively suggested that there is a similarity between the spinal current and the function of the nervous system, the radiations being like the blood, while the less definitely formed circular currents equate with the lymph which, as we know, flows around the body in rather vague channels. Just as these aspects of dense physical body are essential to its life and health, so are the vital currents. The blood and lymph (whose functions overlap) bring nutriment to the tissues and carry away waste products. The nervous system is concerned with regulation and balance of the whole organism.

In the vital field the same threefold functions appear. The spinal current is associated not only with consciousness, but also indirectly with autonomic regulation of the whole field. In the dense body the blood carries chemical material in liquid solution, but the red corpuscles take oxygen to the tissues and bring back carbon dioxide from these and dispose of it. Similarly the radiations in the vital field absorb and carry vitality (*prana*) from the outer atmosphere and dispose of subtle waste matter. The circular currents are like the lymph which is in effect a reservoir of chemical food for the body. Its etheric counterpart is an accumulator of potential vital energy for the whole system.

The physical health and well-being of the individual is

directly linked with the condition of the vital field which, as already said, is a complex structure, but has its own autonomy. It is profoundly influenced both by physical conditions, nutrition, hygiene, etc., but changes in the outer aura, which reflects psychological states, also have a profound influence on the coherence and behavior of this field.

A person who is materially starved or overfed, or poisoned with drugs or smoky air, or insufficient or excessive exercise, suffers from corresponding damage to the vital structure. But his mental attitude to life can equally affect it. One who withdraws from life and refuses to face its problems will gradually develop a colorless aura (thereby justifying the colloquial phrases that "is so colorless", or "so grey"). The vital currents become damped down, life becomes slow, and after a period of time, instead of a glowing structure, the aura looks like a thin grey fog.

Conversely, a person, who is always greedily seeking extraverted experience, strains the aura so that it either consumes itself as a result of overmuch psychological drive, or it is stretched and pulled out of shape by being forced in too many directions at once. In the first case, it tends to perish and become brittle like silk in a lampshade too near a hot electric bulb. In the second, it begins to leak, so that energy which should be kept inside it is dissipated to no useful purpose. Such individuals get ill, the first by sudden exhaustion, the latter by insidious and increasing fatigue.

General ill health shows in the vital field as a whole, but local disease produces marked local changes as well as a disturbance of the whole. Thus a superficial cut or bruise is visible etherically as well as physically. There is a slight break in the rhythm of the vital currents over the site of the injury. Such things as malignant disease or abscess formation show both a generally deranged etheric field and a localized condition. This is often visible long before there is any evidence of organic trouble. It begins as a patch of disorganization of the currents in the particular part of the field over the organ affected. The rhythmic flow becomes broken and irregular, and small vortices form in which, as in a river

whirlpool, waste matter accumulates instead of being thrown
out. The natural color disappears, and the whole texture
becomes denser as the waste material coagulates, just as mud
is deposited by water. The movement slows down until real
stagnation occurs. Then, at a certain point, the whole process
becomes, as it were, precipitated into the level of the physical
tissues and local organic disease is established.

As against the disease due to stagnation, other complaints
begin differently. In these cases—active tuberculosis of the
lungs, for instance—the fabric of the etheric field becomes
markedly overactive and tense. It is stiff and thin and becomes unable to carry its normal quota of energies. Eventually the structure breaks down like a piece of fine material
overstretched. It is at the point when the etheric has broken
that necrosis of tissue and cavitation in the lung occurs.

If we examine the minutiae of tissue and structure from the
vital side it becomes evident that the various currents or
wave lengths of energy in the etheric field play different
parts in their formation. They interact with and counter-
balance one another so that the tissue either grows, remains
healthy, or deteriorates, according to age and general health.

Thus, if we consider bone we see under the ordinary micro-
scope a series of Haversian systems in which a minute blood
vessel is surrounded by concentric tubes of dense, inert bone
substance. Between these tubes are layers of living bone
cells, or osteoblasts and osteoclasts. To the clairvoyant, aside
from the blood in the vessel, the vital pattern of bone appears
to consist of two streams of energy circling in contrary directions round the central channel. Of these, one stream is
constructive or anabolic, the other is destructive or catabolic.
The balance between them determines the condition of the
bony tissue. If the anabolic is strongest, as in children, the
bone grows. If the two are balanced, it is healthy, as in young
adults. When the catabolic energies acquire predominance,
as age increases, the bone tends to degenerate and become
brittle. The same principle probably applies to all tissues
throughout the body except the nervous system.

The latter is a special case because of its association with

consciousness. For in the nervous system there is no increase in the number of cells from the moment they are formed. A man may die with *fewer* than he had at birth, if some have degenerated, but he never has *more* at any time. All that happens is that, as the child develops, more cells are called into activity as required, and this activity is coordinated into more and more complex systems of integrated action.

A nerve cell consists of a body and a fibre which may be several feet long. Thus a cell in the lower part of the spinal cord may be prolonged by its own fibre to the tips of the toes. Looked at from the physiological viewpoint, such a fibre consists of a thread in a fatty myelin sheath. The fibre, as we have said, is continuous from cell to end organ. The sheath, however, is broken up into sections at Ranvier's nodes. To the clairvoyant there is a steady flow of etheric energy of a certain order, which we will call "earthy" or "terrene", from the periphery towards the cell—whether the fibre be motor or sensory. Within that stream impulses of a different and subtler energy level can be observed, flowing towards the cell or away from it according to whether the nerve is sensory or motor. An analogy to what happens is where there is a steady stream of water, and a sound wave from a submerged bell can travel up or down the stream regardless of the direction of the current of the water itself.

Hence a fully functioning nerve always, and even when quiescent, carries a constant stream of its own vegetative, earthy energies which appear to the clairvoyant as a silvery line. A damaged or unhealthy nerve loses its brightness and appears like a thread of grey cotton, without radiance or vitality. When stimulated by outgoing or incoming impulses, it is as if beads of brighter light leap along the fibre from node to node in the sheath.

The latter is in accord with latter-day physiological findings, that nerve impulses travel in a fibre, *not* at the speed of light or electricity (some 180,000 miles per second) as might have been expected from the fact that electrical phenomena occur when a nerve is stimulated, or, conversely, since an electrical impulse will excite a nerve; but only at about 30

feet per second, suggesting a chain of impulses stimulating one part of the nerve after another and taking a little time to do so. Moreover, recent physiological research has suggested that the nodes of Ranvier are more than a structural peculiarity, and that they are definitely connected with the passage of impulses along the fibre.

There is here also an interesting confirmation of the psychic view that the vegetative or terrene correspond to dense matter. For interruption of physical structure of the nerve by injury or disease also interrupts the continuity of this energy stream. The actual nerve impulses do not bridge the gap, which points to the fact that the vegetative energy levels act as a carrier medium for the subtler levels of vitality, at any rate in the nervous system.

The above may seem too detailed to be included in a general description of the vital field of man. But it is mentioned here to suggest the principle of the overall duality of this field.

This duality can best be envisaged as originating in the main spinal current. It should be made clear that there are many forms and levels of energy both in the spine and the nervous system, but to avoid confusion we will only consider them in terms of two main groups. Moreover, we are considering at this point only that which is *vital* in the sense that it is the background to the physical organism: *prana* in the narrower sense.

The field of this spinal current is, as we have said, between crown and sacrum. Between these, as between the two terminals of an alternating current main, there is a pulsating stream of energy. At one moment the pulse moves from below upward, at the next from above down. It can be said that the upward pulse is terrene or earthy, while the other, coming earthy, the other solar.

Using this dualtiy as a principle, the terrene energy phase is that which carries out the chemical activities in the body, while the solar is responsible for the coordination of the chemical matter into physiological life. The two are in reality at one level of energy, but they function as if they were

different, one being linked with the mineral life, the other with the organic being of the individual.

It follows, from what has been said, that the other and subsidiary energies in the vital aura (radiation etc.), being induced from the first, spinal current, will also have two phases to correspond with those in this current—one phase earthy, the other solar.

What has been said above has to do with the inner or health aura as a paraphysiological organism: a subtler counterpart of the physical body. The wider auric field which represents psychological function not only interpenetrates the paraphysiological aura, but also affects it profoundly, inducing in its own energy streams with its own wave lengths.

Thought and feeling, not to mention profounder spiritual activity, are constantly reflected into the health aura, which changes from moment to moment as mental processes take place. There is an Indian saying that "Prana follows thought". This is indeed seen to be a fact because there is an immediate alteration in the health aura as mood and thinking change. Of this more will be said later. For the time being, however, we need to amplify what has been said about the duality of the field, for a pair implies polarization, and polarization implies a third factor—the field between the poles. We have already suggested the vertical polarization in which one phase of the spinal current, and hence of its subsidiaries, can be called solar, while the reverse phase is called terrene or earthy. There is, however, a useful tradition, confirmed by direct observation, which is based on a septenary scheme, and which is an extension of the principle of polarization in a more elaborate form.

This septenary is a principle of occult science applicable to the whole universe known to man. In it there are two triads joined by an intermediate and single level. The system is usually depicted thus:

$$\begin{array}{cc} 1 & 7 \\ 2 & 6 \\ 3 & 5 \end{array}$$
$$4$$

The groups 1, 2, 3 represent one pole, 5, 6, 7 the other; while 4 is the field between them.

Taking this in its simplest form in connection with the present subject, we see the aura as made up of seven levels or main wave lengths of etheric energy. Of these, the first three are linked with psychological and spiritual activity, while the last three are concerned with the physical and chemical processes of the body. The fourth or middle level is an intermediary, and is the bridge over which consciousness plays between the objective physical world and the indwelling individual. It is worth adding that this fourth level is probably that of the chemical atom, which never exists singly for any length of time except in the inert gases (neon, helium, etc.) but always combines at once into molecules of gas, liquid or solid. These latter represent the fifth, sixth and seventh levels of the vital physical world.

This is to shift the emphasis in some of the older writings, in which four etheric levels are described, followed by three of physical matter in gaseous, liquid and solid forms. It is true that allowance is made for the fact that the latter have a certain background of anchored, fixed etheric, of a very different kind from the vital field of living matter. But the picture left in the mind is not quite that of present-day thought, where both direct observation and modern science see only a difference of energy pattern or wave length between energy and matter, and it will facilitate further study to consider the whole physical world, both etheric and dense, as a single but sevenfold field.

For convenience in dealing with the living organism, it will be useful to be able to speak of the subtler (i.e., 1st, 2nd and 3rd) levels as *vital* ethers and the denser as *chemical* (5th, 6th, 7th) or physico-chemical ethers, separated and joined by the fourth level—that of the *chemical* atom. This is also the interface between the conscious individual and his dense body.

It will also be convenient if we link the subtler ethers with the solar energy phase, and the denser with the earthy. For the predominant quality of each of these triads derives from

its basic origin. Yet, as in music each basic note has a series of overtones and undertones, so can every level of the whole septenary field be thought of as, to some extent, infused with the qualities of both solar and earthy energies.

In this way, incarnate man lives in the physical body through a sevenfold field of interrelated energies, of which three are essentially his own and subjective, three belong to the objective physical world, and the middle or fourth in the link between the two. This complex field arranges itself in space into the aura already described, making a form with definite, if mobile, shape and structure. The subtler energies are instantly responsive to the mental states of the individual. The denser energies both affect and are affected by the condition of the physical tissues. Both sets interact on one another, using the fourth, central level as the connection.

Within the aura are the chakras, or force centers, already mentioned in Chapter One. These are of paramount functional importance, as they are in effect the organs by which psycho-spiritual man expresses himself in the etheric, and thence in the dense physical world. Taken collectively, they should be a balanced system, each one of which reflects a certain form of psychic activity; while taken together they are a manifestation of the whole of the individual in action. Nothing of nonphysical man becomes effective in the dense worlds except through the chakras.

If, for instance, the solar plexus chakra becomes paralyzed, whether from psychic inhibition or by the misuse of drugs, etc., emotion will not be felt in physical consciousness, while inhibition of the head centers will cancel the expression of thought or intuition. But the chakra system is so interlocked that if clear thought is paralyzed, say through alcoholic indulgence, primitive emotion and solar plexus activity will be exaggerated.

These are simple instances, but so complex is the significance of the chakras both collectively and individually, that it cannot be gone into further except in a special study involving the whole of man, from the spiritual to the dense physical extremes. One thing can be added, however, which is that

though the chakras are most easily to be seen in the denser part of the vital aura, they actually extend into and through the ovoid or psychic aura, and act as direct channels between the two levels.

There is also an interesting and well-known relation between the chakras and the autonomic and endocrine systems. This is more than merely spacial or anatomical, it is also functional; and when a major endocrine change, such as that of puberty, takes place in the body it is accompanied by—indeed, preceded by—a corresponding change in the chakra balance. For such a stage as puberty goes hand in hand with a change of consciousness, or psychic activity, and the chakras are directly related to the psychic state of the individual.

The chakra system and the endocrine system have certain other features in common apart from their simultaneous function at different times of life. For one thing, all those from the throat down are associated with important nerve centers or junctions, while the controlling key to them, especially in man, is to be found in the head. Thus the pituitary gland is now recognized as the master switch to the rest of the glands, and the corresponding chakra is extremely important with regard to the general balance of the lower centers.

Occult science connects the highest functions of man with the *brahmarandra* or crown chakra and the pineal body. But this is to anticipate the future, and scarcely applies to the average man. The scientist does not consider the pineal as other than a vestigial eye, and has found no hormonal secretion from it. Thus to all intents and purposes the *ajna* or brow chakra and the pituitary gland are the highest center and gland, respectively, fully active in the ordinary human being.

It is interesting to note, also, that the endocrine glands which relate to each chakra are at least dual in function (the pituitary, itself two glands fused into one, being far more complex still); while the chakra, seen clairvoyantly, consists primarily of two interweaving streams of energy running in opposite directions, one of which can be considered as positive or anabolic, the other as negative or catabolic. This also

roughly corresponds to the dual endocrine glands as indicated on the accompanying table, though it should be added that to try and fit these together too closely will show gaps and possible discrepancies in the light of present knowledge, whether of the chakras or of the actual glands.

Correspondences

Crown—Pineal Body. (Not recognized as endocrine.)
Brow—Pituitary.
Throat—Thyroid and Parathyroid.
Heart—Thymus.
Solar Plexus—Adrenals (dual) and pancreas (dual).
Spleen—Spleen. (Not recognized as endocrine.)
Sacrum—Gonads, prostrate, etc.

It seems probable, too, that there is a relationship between parts of the central nervous system and the chakras, and hence the endocrine glands too. Modern work on the hypothalamus and the floor of the third ventricle of the brain may be revealing in connection with the autonomic system, perhaps showing it as the place where the parasympathetic and sympathetic nervous, as against the endocrine systems are controlled and balanced. Already, it may be suggested that the superior parasympathetic—i.e., vagal—system may derive from this region, blending from above with the sympathetic, whose brain is the solar plexus (more accurately called the coeliac plexus, which includes the solar and lunar ganglia). At the opposite end of the body, the sacral parasympathetic rises to meet the sympathetic and to balance with this, and there is a suggestive point connected with the psychic view of the polarity of the spinal current, between head and sacrum, and hence between the essentially human creative and the animal sexual creative centers.

It is only to be expected that the shape and behavior of the chakras and the pattern of their detailed structure will also vary, not only with the general change of conscious expression shown in different stages of life, but also from moment to moment according as the individual is actively engaged in thought, in meditation, or feeling strongly about a situation.

Thus, in a baby, where consciousness is slight and simple, the chakras show only as slight depressions on the outer surface of the health aura. From the center of this cup a thin stalk runs to the spinal cord or to the particular nerve center to which the chakra corresponds. Later, however, as conscious activity develops and enriches they become deeper, wider, and, moreover, project beyond the general surface of the health aura. Further, though in the baby, which is psychically wide open to its environment, there is no adequate covering to the depressed cup. In the mature chakra, working healthily, there is a membrane of etheric material which covers the mouth of the cornucopia-like organ and serves as a filter for impressions from the psychic world, and does not allow everything to pass through into physical consciousness.

It is only where a particular chakra has been damaged, or where the corresponding aspect of the individual's psyche has not developed, that this membrane is malformed or incomplete. Such damage can occur from shock, prolonged use of drugs, mediumistic practices, unwise meditation, hatha yoga breathing exercises, etc. In the first cases it is most likely to affect the solar plexus, in the second it may be the head centers which are affected. But any other center may equally become improperly protected through misuse or accident.

Unbalanced psychic development is a somewhat different matter, because there the chakra is likely to have remained in a more or less infantile state and never to have developed to its proper shape. Thus a highly intellectual person who has remained emotionally infantile, may have a labile, shallow, unprotected solar plexus chakra which leaves him a prey to hysteria and lack of control. One who may be very intelligent, but who has no creative ability, may find himself with an immature throat center, and hence liable to temporary loss of voice, while his usual voice may be thin and superficial even if not high pitched. Functional heart troubles may equally be linked with the corresponding chakra, and be associated with the inability to love. A sensation of burning up the spine may be due to the sacral center having been damaged by sexual aberrations. And so on.

The chakras are thus a most important part of the etheric organism, for it is through them that the psychic or vital ethers enter the field and balance the denser, earthy or chemical energies in making or marring physical health. In this, while proper physical food and hygiene are essential to tissue *structure*, so are psychic and spiritual stability and integration to tissue *function*, the two—structure and function—causing health or disease according to whether they are or are not balanced.

3

The Process of Incarnation: Fertilization

The word *incarnation* means, literally, descent into flesh. Hence, in this chapter we propose to consider what happens when the human spirit and soul acquire an earthly body. Doubtless, were we able to see so far, we should find that there is a preparatory stage at the psychic levels, comparable to that of gestation at the physical. Individual human evolution has always been described as a journey, and when one is going to leave one's home—which in this case is taken to be at the spiritual level—certain arrangements have to be made beforehand, while the journey itself involves movement from stage to stage before the goal—the physical world—is reached. We know little or nothing about these earlier phases of incarnation, though Eastern literature gives some general hints, in terms of the activation or reactivation of certain seeds of personality at the mental and emotional levels. These are called imperishable germs by H. P. Blavatsky, permanent atoms by Besant and Leadbeater and correspond to *prajna* in Hindu writings. This, however, is not the concern of our study, the subject of which is the physical etheric level only.

Some suggestions will be made here as to how man acquires the use of his physical vehicle. The material, although linked with traditional ideas, is based on clairvoyant investigation. Hence, it must be taken, at best, as incomplete; at worst, as illusory but in any case as symbolic.

Most biologists today recognize a purpose behind evolution. They see life as developing along many lines, some of which go into blind alleys and hence to extinction of a species, but others which are successful lead from a lower to a higher biological level, and so represent evolution. The origin and

goal of the purposive, teleological drive is undefined. Some call it life, others use the time honored word God. But these words are general and may be said to represent a beginning and an end, leaving the middle vague. Yet whatever the intelligence behind evolution, this must clearly apply as much to the middle and active stages as to origins and ultimates. Moreover, it seems to specialize itself and to subserve the individual parts of the evolving world in such a way that rivalry or cooperation of the most awe-inspiring kind become evident. Many phenomena bear out the idea of "nature, red in tooth and claw", others show a commercial acumen worthy of the City of London. One cannot envisage the partnership between shark and pilot fish; between a certain jellyfish and the decoy fish who lures others to their death, and then lives literally on the crumbs falling from its superior's table —while himself escapes death; and even the cyclic phases of life involving bacteria, plants and animals, without feeling that there is active intelligence at work. If this is so, it fits in with universal beliefs. For in all communities, at all times, there has been folklore relating to invisible, psychic entities connected with Nature. We have everywhere stories of fairies, gnomes, sylphs, local gods, and beyond them hierarchies of greater gods and angels, all of which act as intermediaries between the greatest God and His creatures. In Hindu literature they are called generally *Devas*—a term we shall use in order to avoid the limited connotations of the Christian term *angel* as conceived (or forgotten) in most churches.

Such agents or devas are naturally accepted and known to most psychically sensitive people, who recognize them as more than merely images projected by their own or other people's minds and see them as *entia per se*: things or creatures existing in their own right, just as birds and animals do, save that they have no dense physical bodies. A famous Western psychologist was once asked whether he thought that fairies, elementals and all such creatures perceived in dreams and visions were only products of the imagination, or whether they had a foundation in objective reality. His an-

swer was to the effect that if they had not the latter we should not be able to imagine them, however much we may humanize them by adapting the form in which we see them to our own mental habits.*

This may seem to the modern scientist a digression from our subject, and completely fantastic. It suggests a return to the animism of primitive peoples. And so, in a certain sense, it is. But whereas the savage feels himself at the mercy of the invisible powers of nature, many civilized men see nature as a place of law and order, which becomes less and less of a menace as they understand that law. Hence this animism is sophisticated and deliberate, and only resembles that of the primitive in thinking of life as itself both organized and intelligent. It, nevertheless, has an important bearing on what follows. For in the process of building all natural objects, the deva hierarchy plays a most important part, in a way little understood by anybody, and completely unrecognized by science.

Those entities which help in the formation and maintenance of the physical body belong to orders whose normal habitat in the psychic world is on the confines of the dense physical in the region we speak of as vital etheric. In plant and animal life—unless interfered with by man—this role is entirely automatic, and manifests in terms of instinctive behavior, though this represents only the superficial aspects of devic activity. The deeper side shows itself in cell life, and even beyond, in the complex field of mineral and atomic existence. In man, however, there is the additional and complicating element of the human mind and what it contains in the way of self-consciousness and relative freewill. These give man a certain power of imposing himself—for better or worse—on the natural, instinctive devic pattern.

The subject of deva hierarchy is a study in itself. Even the limited field of the relationship between the human and devic

---

*The reader may want to read about the cooperation between man and devas THE SECRET LIFE OF PLANTS by Peter Tompkins and other works on the Findhorn (Scotland) Community founded by Peter and Eileen Caddy.

kingdom is a vast subject, as yet practically untouched. For the moment it will suffice if we suggest a main division between *Arupa,* or Formless Devas whose realm is that we speak of as spiritual, and *Rupa* or Form Devas—a lower order of intelligence—which live and work in the personal or material world. Below the Rupa Deva are further levels of still lower entities of more or less permanent form, known as elementals. Where man in concerned there is an interaction between himself and the devas which may be cooperative or, on the other hand, conflicting. In any case, the two orders of being, the human and the devic, appear to be entirely complementary in the scheme of things, and may be looked upon as two dimensions of life running at right angles to one another.[1]

In biology the smallest unit of organic matter is the gene, which makes up the chromosomes on which all reproduction and heredity depend. It is now thought that a gene is an asymmetric chemical molecule of vast complexity. The lack of symmetry gives rise to the power of mutation which has long puzzled biologists, and seems to represent the occasional changing of the intramolecular patterns.

It would appear that the devic element in evolution makes its prime impact on living matter through the genes. The gene itself, being chemical, belongs to the terrene triad of the septenary, but it is activated by finer forces belonging to the solar triad, working through the critical fourth level. This level is like the core of an electrical transformer. and the energies are here "stepped down" or up in the same manner. In this instance, however, the core is not merely a passive, mechanical element, but an active factor, which shapes and directs the energies into the chemical levels of genes and chromosomes according to a prearranged pattern. That is,

---

[1] It would probably be more accurate to say that man and deva each represent two dimensions of a three-dimensional world, so that each kingdom has two dimensions of its own and one held in common with the other. This, however, is a more complicated picture and need not be elaborated further here. See P. D. Bendit, *The Sacred Flame*, Theosophical Publishing House, London.

the devic intelligences act at this level rather like a lantern slide in a beam of light, or more exactly, since the pattern moves and changes, a cinema film, in which the light energy becomes modified as it goes through the film, throwing on to the screen a living, changing picture. But one has to go yet a step further than this analogy, and conceive of the screen itself changing as the pattern thrown upon it changes in accordance with a certain sequence of events in time, so that the zygote grows and develops in the way we know.

Looking at the devic kingdom, it can be said that it holds the dynamic blueprints of natural evolution, and is the agent of their fulfilment— as a builder carries out the instructions of the architect through his own activities and those of his subordinates. This would also probably account for the sporadic deviations we call mutations, though how and for what reason these occur is a mystery.

Leaving aside detailed study of the subhuman kingdoms, we come now to a consideration of man. For he is a special case in that all that applies to subhuman nature applies to himself but he brings with him an extra element, his own individuality. Each man, in the technical occult sense, is a Monad, coming into incarnation in order to make his latent individuality actual and explicit. This individuality may be incipient and largely latent in any incarnation—as in most primitive races still existent— or it may be considerably developed and particularized, as in the outstanding personalities which are at once unique and yet belong more to man as a whole than to any particular race or nation. Thus we have in each human being the seed at least of something which is his, and his only, and which, scarcely so much as germinal in the early stages, nevertheless consistently develops along a teleological path already implicit in the germ from the beginning.

Though it may seem early to speak of this, yet on it depends the whole of what follows. If we realize that the human Monad is constantly endeavoring to express itself fully in space and time by incarnating in the material world, we have a key to the cipher of physical life. It is, as it were, trying to

sound its own unique and individual note in a universe which muffles and distorts it, creating discord and disharmony. But as, through understanding, it overcomes the seeming resistance of nature, the individual note begins to rouse more and more over- and undertones in the material of which the personality consists. In this way the original single note of the Monad becomes enriched and clarified so that the developed man may be looked upon as sounding a complex chord which is an integral part of the total symphony of life.

The reason for introducing such a concept at this point is that in the process of human incarnation a factor is involved which is absent in subhuman procreation. In the latter we can see the polarity of the male and female cells at work under the direction of the devic agencies. In man, however, there is an overshadowing of all three by the human Monad or individuality. This individuality, weak or strong, is a permanent factor which plays upon and modifies the etheric field in all its sevenfold aspects, throughout the whole of life. Hence, the quality and type of the vital etheric field, and consequently of the body itself, is influenced more or less profoundly from the first moment of fertilization of the ovum, by the individuality of the incarnating Monad.

"To him that overcometh, to him will I give . . . a white stone, and in that stone a new name written which no one knoweth but he that receiveth it."[2] This passage can be interpreted—among many other interpretations—as signifying that when the human spirit overcomes the resistance and obstacles in incarnation and acquires a physical body, it then becomes "named" and hence purely individual. The difficulties and objections to such incarnation in matter—for such it is when looked at from the freedom of the spiritual world—is suggested in books like *The Secret Doctrine* and in the first chapter of Genesis. All tradition has it that temptation in some form had to be placed before the Monad before it could be lured onto the difficult and perilous path of active physical evolution.

---

[2] Rev. 2:17.

Bearing this in mind, we can now consider what takes place at the time of human procreation. Sexual intercourse normally involves a momentary fusion of the vital aspects of the participants. The depth of this will depend on the emotional and mental rapport of the pair. Afterwards each becomes once more discrete, save that a magnetic tie is made which may be deep and lasting or may be superficial and ephemeral. This is the case with the most casual relationship, and is an important reason for the psychic confusion which is nearly always a cause of unhappiness among the promiscuous. If fertilization results, the link becomes stronger and more enduring even if—as happens in many cases, at least as regards the man—it remains unconscious. The partners in the sex act may separate and never meet again, but there is a bond between them where their respective germ plasm is fused in the body of a child. It is because of the common germ plasm that it is very nearly impossible for close blood relations to be entirely objective about one another, and this tie persists even after all the psychological accumulation of stored and shared experience have been consciously made clear.

The biological phenomena associated with fertilization are common knowledge. From the psychic angle a whole series of events takes place. It is as if when the act occurs, which will result in the creation of a body, the attention of a human Monad were attracted, perhaps only momentarily. Where and how that Monad or individual spirit exists is a matter outside the scope of this book, and it is again one of the greatest mysteries about the mysterious creature we call man. But it is as if on the fusion of ovum and sperm cell a response were to come from the depths of the universe so that the resulting zygote at once becomes the physical focus for the incarnation of a particular Monad.

It is a principle of occultism that when one speaks of man at the spiritual—monadic or sub-monadic (Egoic) level—one is at the same time speaking of the world of Arupa Devas, and in particular of those called in *The Secret Doctrine,* and by E. L. Gardner the *Asuras* or Luciferians, the Dhyan Buddhas

and the Dhyan Chohans. Hence the response of the spiritual human element involves of necessity that of the spiritual (arupa) devic aspect too. Few people as yet realize that, while at the rupa or form levels, deva and man are complementary, at the arupa or spiritual levels they are not complementary but actually one.

At this point, no adequate description can be given in simple or biological or psychic terms, so we can only use a language which is at least in one aspect symbolic and analogic. Let us consider the process of incarnation in terms of geometry, and in particular of the tetrahedron, the simplest of the Platonic solids. We can symbolize animal procreation as a triangle, horizontal and at earth level. Each angle of the triangle represents one of the three factors; the male, the female and the rupa devic. In the field of the triangle the embryo takes shape.

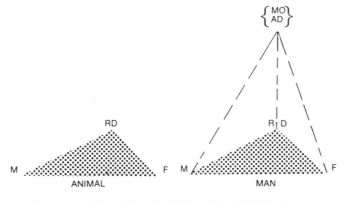

Diagram I. M=Male. F=Female. RD=Rupa Deva. MO=Monad.
AD=Arupa Deva.

In man, however, we introduce a third dimension, placing the Monad at the apex, whence it plays down the sides and edges of the figure on to the physical level triangle, creating a magnetic field between itself and its potential body. The devic aspect connected with the Monad is what is called (in *The Secret Doctrine*) Luciferian, indicating that it belongs to the plane of the Will or Atma. There is also a rupa deva in

charge of the actual building operations at the earth level. The latter is an agent of the Atmic, Luciferian deva—the clerk of the works under the architect.

The clairvoyant equivalent of this mental analogy can only be put in inadequate terms which do not make sense from the scientific viewpoint. They are, therefore, only to be taken principally as imaginative pictures.

It has been observed a number of times that it is as if at the first touch of monadic influence the Arupa Deva bends a ray of light into a horizontal circle at the etheric level, thus defining the field. Into its center he drops, on the end of a golden thread, a minute spinning disc of intense golden light, a miniature sun. This is actually a reactivation of the permanent atom or imperishable germ at the physical level from the latency in which it lies between incarnations. It is not the zygote. The Deva itself, like the Monad, does not descend directly into the field, but remains in its own world. The golden nucleus, as it spins, sends out radiations which induce and set into motion material of the whole septenary field of energy. This, by a process of magnetic attraction becomes an intricate pattern of interweaving currents moving at great speed. This pattern is an individual one, and is determined by the nature of the Monad itself. This gradually assumes the form of a three-dimensional sphere. In septenary terms, the fourth is at the center of the sphere, and at the many points of intersection of the several currents.

It has been noted that the physical and microscopic zygote is not, at first, within the circular field. The reason for this may be that what has been described is concerned with human evolution, and the incarnation of a human individual mind and spirit. The zygote itself is purely animal, and belongs to the terrene level. Hence, for a short time the complex field first described is held suspended psychically if not spacially above the zygote, at the first etheric level, where the circular stage of the field manifests. Many zygotes die at once. But as soon as a magnetic link is established between it and the circular field, germination begins. This draws the germ and the field spacially together, until the zygote—by

now probably at the morula or blastula stage—and the central nucleus of spinning energy coincide. It is during this process that the circle becomes a sphere, the outer surface of which acts as a protective skin, a ring-pass-not, for the embryonic growth. We have thus a psychic womb within the physical womb, as suggested in cryptic form in occult writings. This secondary womb or cocoon corresponds to the placenta and membranes which are at first part of the embryo but which are destined to be discarded at birth.

These phenomena, though described in language which may be largely symbolic, nevertheless appear to take place at a particular point in space and a moment in time. One hesitates to speak of them in terms of physical size or duration. Nevertheless, it appears as if in spatial terms, the circular field is at first roughly an inch across, and is to be found in the region of the etheric counterpart of the uterus. The fertilization of the ovum is known to take place outside the uterus, and probably in one of the Fallopian tubes, where it begins to proliferate, reaching the uterine cavity in its early morula or blastula phase. It is then brought spacially as well as magnetically into position, as regards both the physical uterus and the etheric field. The spherical form of the field is established at the stage where the embryonic amnion and chorion become defined—the protective etheric skin corresponding to these membranes.

Up to this point the embryo has had no particular characteristics other than those brought by the genes—the external heredity. At this stage, however, a certain pattern is imposed upon it from within—one relative to the needs of the incoming individuality. The selection of that pattern is another mystery, but it seems to involve less the addition of active factors than the deletion or inhibition of some of the potentialities in the genes. In this way the full possibilities of the individual are not allowed to develop. It is as if certain things were selected for use during the ensuing life, while others are kept in abeyance. The exact mechanism of this is beyond our comprehension except in general terms, representing the intelligent workings of the law of karma in the physiological sphere.

Thus when a person is born into a family whose heredity gives him a very small or over large physique which is bitterly resented, one can presume that this is an example of karmic reaping of what has been sown in some other phase of existence. This also explains why certain people are born into families suffering from hereditary and congenital diseases. It applies still more to such individual congenital failures of development as lead to cleft palate, clubfoot and other deformities which are individual and not familial. The actual point of impact of the selection is through the permanent atoms or imperishable germs, the enduring foci of the Monad at each of the main levels or planes of the material worlds. It is probably that the spinning core of the etheric field is a manifestation of activity around the physical imperishable germ. But the check put on the unrestricted development of this activity is due mainly to the interference of the devic agents of karma, known in Sanskrit as *Nirmanakayas,* or Lords of Karma.

This concludes the first phase of incarnation. The zygote is by now embedded in the uterine wall, having been drawn into position not only by the obvious physiological mechanism of the ciliated epithelium of the Fallopian tube, but also by the magnetic pull of the circular etheric field. It now enters the second phase of intra-uterine growth in which the zygote becomes the vehicle of a human Monad and its psyche.

4

The Process of Incarnation:
Quickening and Birth

In the months which follow impregnation and the embedding of the zygote in the uterine wall, it develops through the well-known physical stages. Step by step the mass of tissues which results from cell division becomes differentiated. At the same time, function begins to arise in the tissues, and within a few weeks nerve fibres can be excited and movement of muscle occurs. Bit by bit these primitive elements of function become so coordinated and organized that the body acts as a whole. The phenomenon known as *quickening,* which takes place about the middle of pregnancy, does not, from the physiological angle, appear to represent any special moment of fetal development. It is then that the mother first becomes aware of movement in the womb, and hence quickening is looked upon as a purely maternal, subjective incident.

From the psychic angle, the earlier stages represent the activity of the rupa devas and elementals, building the etheric structure in which the physical form is developed, following the general patterns representing early stages of animal evolution. In that sense the embryo is not yet really human. The incoming human individual hovers above the growing body at his own psychic level. He is not yet consciously linked to it, perhaps not even aware of it. The link, however, is stabilized by the mediation of the Arupa Deva, who is a partial reflection of the individual spirit. At the quickening, however, it seems that the human individual becomes, perhaps for the first time, attentive to what is taking place in the vehicle he is to inhabit. It is as if the weight of this body were now such that he feels the drag of it, and is compelled to look down, and for the first time to pay

attention to it. At this moment, a *new ray* of vital energy flashes into the embryonic field. This is the first direct projection of the human Monad into the growing body, and belongs to the solar, spiritual triad of energies. These correspond to the superior principles Atma, Buddhi, and Manas which correspond to Will, Wisdom, and Creative Activity (the spiritual trinity in man). It may be this sudden vivification which draws the mother's attention to the fact that she has indeed a *live* baby in her womb. Doubtless there is at this point a moment of special concentration from the incoming individual on to the fetus—just as an electric light may shine more brightly for a moment of increased voltage, when first switched on. But just as the bulb would be damaged were this pressure to be maintained for long, so the individual to some extent withdraws again without, however, losing complete touch with his body while its development proceeds further. Psychologists have ample evidence of prenatal consciousness among their patients, some of whom directly, and some indirectly and symbolically, prove that they were in a primitive manner aware of intra-uterine conditions and events. This fits in with the above, showing that the germ of self-consciousness at the physical level exists before the actual time of birth.

The relationship between the maternal etheric field and that of the fetus is, clearly, very intimate though each is largely discrete. The only direct interchange between the two is similar to that in the placental villi, which are bathed in the mother's blood, where they absorb nutriment, oxygen— and perhaps drugs—and excrete the fetal waste products into it for her to dispose of through her own excretory mechanism. There is a selective filtration between the maternal and the fetal blood, but no direct mixing of them, as the fetus grows its own blood cells, just as it grows the cells of other and fixed tissues. The etheric fields act on one another in a similar selective manner.

The mother and the child are separate beings, yet in very close contact. Consequently, just as the toxins and drugs in the mother's blood may affect the fetus, so do her emotional

and vital states. If she does not want the child, and is un-
happy or frightened, these feelings alter her own vital field,
and by contagion cause effects in the child's. Similarly, just as
a physical trauma to the mother can damage the fetus, so
may a psychological shock react on the child, possibly to the
extent of affecting the actual development of tissue. Thus
consideration from the psychic angle of the *mechanical* processes of gestation and babyhood confirm and explain what is
known to the psychologist in terms of *function*.

The unborn child is thus subjected from the first to a series
of forces: (1) The inner selectiveness of the karmic pattern.
This reflects into (2) the hereditary factors in the genes which
are to give him a physical etheric organism, and which
determine the features of the body, its general build, its
susceptibility to certain diseases, the quality of the physical
nervous system, etc., and into (3) the impact of his mother's
physical, psychic and spiritual condition, as reflected into her
own vital field, and the effect of all this on the nutrition of his
own. (This, in addition to the direct psychic influence of her
thoughts and feelings on his own psyche at levels above the
etheric-physical.) The father's influence at this stage is less
important. It plays immediately on the child only through
the genes, which make a direct link between every parent
and evey child.

These three factors represent at this stage the totality of
the karma of the individual for the incipient incarnation,
and, in this sense, are created produced, and brought together, by none other than himself. They are the causes of the
congenital and fundamental texture of the etheric, and hence
of the physical body. They are in nature of the architect's
drawings put into execution by the building contractors—in
this case, elemental entities working under a rupa deva
foreman.

Birth takes place at a moment of time which is highly
significant to the individual. There is a synchronicity between the state of things in the world, and indeed in the
universe, and the instant when the incoming monad comes

into direct relationship with it.* As he emerges from his mother's body, both the physical membranes and the etheric cocoon which have prevented direct contact between himself and the outside world are left behind, discarded. Therefore, he is for the first time unprotected, both psychically and physically. The impact of light and air—usually relatively cold—causes an immediate toning-up, and increase of tension in the etheric, which draws back on itself like a sea anemone when it is touched, and at once assumes a more defined form in relation to the dense body. The movement is precisely the same as is observed later when a shock is received—and confirms the Freudian doctrine of birth representing a traumatic experience.

Birth coincides also with the first breath, which alters both the hydrodynamic balance of the blood circulation and the circulation of vital energy. At this instant the Monad takes formal possession of its body, which has now become truly that of a human being, charged not only with animal vitality but with subtler human energies. The two triads of etheric energies now firmly establish their interplay at and through the fourth etheric level. It may perhaps have some occult significance that at this moment the human child usually cries out, using the voice which later becomes speech and is one of the main differences between men and the lower animals—though it must be admitted that not all authorities would agree on this.

This essay being only about the vital or etheric aspect of man, many other aspects of incarnation are not touched upon. This is not because they are any less important. In fact they are more general and have a greater scope. But if one wishes to understand many of the less obvious problems of health, disease, behavior, and psychological and physiological well-being, it is essential to have a grasp of how and why the etheric organism becomes what it is.

---

*Jung and Pauli, *The Interpretation of Nature and the Psyche.* (Kegan Paul, London.)

5

The First Phase: Childhood

It is common knowledge that the unborn child recapitulates in his body the early history of physical evolution through the animal kingdom. He does this only in broad outline, omitting details, and going through stages representing the various kingdoms from the single-celled protozoan to the mammalian vertebrate. It is less widely recognized, however, that, from birth, he does the same thing as regards the history of man. He passes in his first years from a stage below that of the most primitive savage still extant today up to that of the race to which he now belongs.*

The first phase of a child's life lies between birth and an age given by occult tradition as seven, by orthodox psychologists as five. In practice the physical age at which this stage ends varies, some children reaching the critical point much earlier, others much later than these figures. It seems to be an individual matter; and certainly, if as it sometimes happens, there is a quick reincarnation, in which the psyche (astro-mental organism) of one life is projected into another body without a long dormant period, it is likely to be early. In other cases for reasons unknown, it may be late: a thing which does not by any means denote mental deficiency or backwardness. The point at which this stage of childhood ends is a subtle differentiation in the child's mind, when he first begins to

---

*The Doman-Delacato method has definitively tied this principle to their research and attribute many reading and learning difficulties to an interruption caused when small children are kept from creeping and crawling. Among their works are *What To Do About Your Brain Injured Child,* Glenn Doman (Doubleday, 1964); *Neurological Organization,* Earl Delacato, (C. C. Thomas, 1973); and *Neuro-Psychological Approach,* C. Delacato, (C. C. Thomas, 1971) which clearly explains their theory and work.

realize himself as an individual, separate from his environment.

At birth the etheric field is almost colorless and uncoordinated, yet the potentiality of both color and organization are
there, and can be recognized by the trained percipient. In
fact, both the color and the degree of coordination vary from
moment to moment, as the attention of the child becomes
focused or recedes in diffuse awareness of general conditions.
It is as if when interest in something is aroused, and
consciousness becomes outward-turned, and focused on the
object of interest, the etheric, which has hitherto been somewhat loose and vaguely formed, becomes for the moment
more tense and sharply defined, especially round the head.
Moreover, its opalescent quality becomes suffused with
brighter light and color which, while still faint, show definite
tints. Once more the aurora borealis comes to mind. When
attention is relaxed the etheric returns to its previous state,
except that some slight residue is left from the experience
which permanently adds to its quality and resilience. These
accretions to the fabric of the etheric are indications of progressive mental development—or, more exactly, of the impact of the mind on the etheric field.

Moreover, each child clearly has in itself from the beginning a latent pattern of its future development. Clairvoyant
examination of the etheric, as well as intuitive assessment of
the new-born baby, entirely confirm the psychological view of
congenital conditioning of the child's mind. In other words, a
child is an individual from the moment he is born, and in fact
from the moment he is conceived, and long before this. It is
useless for parents to have fixed ideas as to the child they
want to have—a dancer, an artist, a soldier or a states-man.
The child can only be what he *is*, and can only develop
successfully on *his* own lines. The parent who tries to think
or will his child into a particular set pattern is in grave
danger of doing damage to it. On the other hand, parents who
do not *demand*, but rather, *invite* a certain type of child, are
acting quite legitimately. They may indeed invoke the incarnation of the kind of individual they prefer into the body they

provide. A musical family, for instance is far less likely to wish for a soldier than for another musician or artist; and this, more than heredity, may attract a sensitive, perceptive, individual into their midst. And he, because he is born into a family where the etheric fields of the parents are already sensitive and highly tuned, in turn, will profit from both the environment and the heredity he acquires.

A great deal of the child's reactions during this early stage will depend on the type of his vital field, and more especially of its subtler aspects, those connected with the nervous system and with consciousness. The exact pattern of this field, as we have indicated, is individual, but, for practical purposes we can describe three principal types.

First there is the insensitive type whose earthy energies are very strong, and so give the whole fabric toughness. This, while it shuts him away from much subtle perception, nevertheless protects him from many shocks and strains. This child is a strong little animal who rejoices in violent movement and stimulation. The type corresponds approximately to the *endomorph* in Sheldon's classification.

At the other end of the scale there is the highly strung, hypersensitive child, whose etheric is tense and brittle, the subtle energies being more powerful than the earthy. Hence the physique is apt to be delicate, health precarious, and unable to stand much strain. The child suffers acutely from sudden things, such as being snatched up by an adult, from unaccustomed and unexpected loud noises like fireworks or the banging of a door. It overreacts to medicine or to food, and is nearly always of the allergic type. Sleep is often restless and easily disturbed. This kind of child is usually intelligent, and may conceal its many fears under a bold front, but only at the cost of a great deal of effort and strain. It is highly perceptive, yet often quite unconscious of both its perceptions and its emotions. Hence when ordinary things become too much for it, it generally breaks down into hysterical crying or a fit of temper. This child invariably has a receptive psychic temperament, and the impacts of the nonphysical world are as keenly felt as those of the physical. It is apt to suffer

acutely in childhood, no matter how loving and careful its upbringing. It can be said to correspond to the *ecotomorph*.

The third is an intermediate, relatively balanced type. There is no marked preponderance of one set of energies over the other. The etheric is at once firm enough to be protective, and pliable enough to be sensitive, so that if it receives a shock its natural resilience quickly comes to the rescue and restores balance and serenity. It is, in short, a much more stable type than the second, yet more alert and aware than the first. It is akin to the *mesomorphic* type of Sheldon.

At birth a child becomes physically separate from its mother, and comes into direct contact with its physical environment. But during gestation it has lived enveloped in the psychic environment of its mother. Psychic and physical birth do not coincide. In fact, the separation is not, and should not be, psychically complete at physical birth. It is generally accepted that breast feeding is the best thing for a child, if only from the psychological viewpoint. Next to this, if breast feeding is impossible, the child should be fed on the mother's knee because, it is said, the actual handling of the body is important in developing response to physical sensation, and so eases the incoming Self into its bodily home. Impersonal feeding in a buggy or crib deprives the child both of the sensational and the psychic contact and experience which it needs.

From the psychic viewpoint, breast feeding not only gives milk but also etheric vitality. Failing this, however, close proximity between the child's body and its mother's makes up to some extent on the vital side for any lack of physical nutriment. A nurse who genuinely loves a child also helps on the vital side, but there is not the same close link as there is with the actual mother, through the germ plasm if through nothing else. Thus, in all cases, the mother can give something which no other can give. But if she is an undesirable person, and especially if—as can happen—she really hates the baby; or, equally, if she is morbidly attached to it—which is common—she may harm it as an impersonal nurse does not. In general terms, the person with whom the child feels

most emotional security is the best person to handle it. Thus there is a bias towards the actual mother which must be set off against a possibly more humanly desirable nurse. This is because of the psychic interplay already established at the moment of conception. It is especially strong during the early months or years, whether it is positive or negative. It is only later that others can, and frequently do, advantageously replace the mother, unless there is an innate genuine antipathy between the two. When the psychological development of the individual, now well incarnated in his body, becomes less concerned with the bodily, earthy side of its nature which is derived from its parents, and especially from its mother, the importance of the psychic link with the physical parents diminishes.

Whatever its type, the etheric field of every child is for some years entirely open, and hence vulnerable to the atmosphere in which it has to live. The physical conditions of a home may be poor and shabby, and even physically unhealthy. These may affect its *physical* health, but an atmosphere of warmth and real love will inevitably protect the child from *psychic* strain and tension and help it to grow up emotionally secure and unafraid of life. On the other hand, ideal physical conditions, where there is no deep or true love between the parents, or where inharmonious elements intrude in the form of nurses, servants, or relatives, make the environment insecure and restless. Adults often think that if a child does not hear or see quarrels, or that if the parents do not openly show their unhappiness, fear, or resentment, it knows nothing about them. Nothing could be more misleading. It may be so as far as the child's consciousness is concerned, but such is its psychic sensitivity that it is invaded by the conditions of the psychic atmosphere, and unconsciously reacts to them in a manner depending on temperament. One child will retreat into a cocoon, and become remote and fanciful; another will have vague fears; yet another will have unaccountable fits of tantrums or fretfulness. Some children will even become physically ill, and another type will wet the bed whenever its elders have a crisis in their relationships.

This natural vulnerability is due to the fact that the child is yet neither psychically nor psychologically consciously differentiated from its environment. "I" and "not-I" do not yet exist for it, so that external and internal events, whether in its body or its mind, are inextricably confused. In terms of etheric anatomy, its psychic centers—the chakras—are open and unprotected, like the windows of a house before the glass is put it. Thus an adult exploding in a sudden burst of feeling such as rage shocks the whole of the child's etheric field, and has much the same effect on it as physical shock has on the physical organism; while grief and depression in another person are contagious, and can swamp the child's aura like a fog through an open door.

The closer the blood tie, the greater the effect, for reasons already given. Hence, while the immediate family is important, the father, and particularly the mother, are most important of all. A substitute mother—a nurse or an adoptive mother—is never as psychically close to the child as the real mother, because there is no common germ plasm, and there has never been the same intimate etheric contact. But if she has had charge of the child from its early days, because of the emotional ties which arise, she makes for herself a psychic position in which what she does and is will profoundly affect it. If she is warmhearted and emotionally generous she can fill much of the vacuum left around the child. But she cannot, in the law of things, fill the particular gap which has been left inside the child should its mother desert it. This is a point of particular relevance where children are adopted.

The tie through the germ plasm is one which has been insufficiently recognized in psychology. For it is such that it is, to all intents and purposes, impossible for near blood relations to be entirely objective about one another so long as they are alive; it may happen when the body and its germ plasm is dead, provided all psychological identifications have been resolved, but not before. Hence the parents of a child always have a subtle, underground channel through which they can influence it, while others such as foster-parents have only the one avenue, which is in the psychological

relation between the two. This, as it becomes established, can make a psychic-etheric link of a different order from that with the physical parents whose subterranean influence persists even if there is no psychological or physical contact. It acts as if it were a carrier wave, as used in broadcasting, and conveys the "sound" of the parents' thoughts and feelings into the highly receptive and vulnerable personal field of the child. This is not always an obvious fact, and it naturally differs in degree. But it explains why many parents who honestly refrain from trying to direct the child into the pattern they wish for may very well do so tacitly and even unknown to themselves. It seems highly probably that this is often the cause of the sense of guilt (known in Freudian psychology as the super-ego) in many a sensitive person to whom no harsh word has ever been spoken.

This point is strongly emphasized here because the old adage that "blood is thicker than water" appears to be true, however indifferent the modern mind may be to family ties.

These ties exist even where physical proximity and hence psychological impacts of the ordinary kind do not directly influence the child. They remain inherent in the psychic field, whatever the physical distance between parent and child.

Thus, while the child's reactions to environment, both physical and psychic, rest on its own individual and unique pattern, these develop well or ill according to the environment in which it lives. This is especially the case during this first, pre-egoic phase of life. The general temperament and quality of the etheric field, reflecting the psycho-spiritual man, tends to produce typical reactions to given circumstances. But it must be realized that this typical reaction may be masked by over activity caused by mental factors. Thus a sensitive child may for a time act the tomboy and indulge in rough-and-tumble play, but if it is allowed to go on too long there comes a time when his store of earthy energy runs out and it may then collapse into a sudden illness or into psychological distress. But equally, a stolid earthy type of whom too much intellectual prowess is expected may find

itself unable to cope, and so appears more backward and stupid than it really is.

Such reactions are nature's attempt to restore a balance of vital forces, and much will depend on the inner resources of the child, quite apart from any external remedy which may have to be applied to it, in his difficulties. For its etheric structure is basically entirely individual, and adapted to its individual temperament. It is only when psychic and physical stresses upset the equilibrium that difficulties occur.

Thus, from the first, the child depends for its welfare on a proper interplay between its innate self and its environment. If it is well-adjusted, the various currents and levels of vital energy weave themselves into a strong and resilient structure, even if it is of the highly sensitive type. And as experience accumulates the whole etheric gives an appearance of soft brilliance which is markedly different from that of the early pearl-grey appearance of the new-born baby.

As the child becomes increasingly self-conscious there is a progressive but radical change in the etheric aura, especially about the head. It becomes clear and defined in a way the preconscious child is not. It must be added here that certain children seem to be self-conscious from birth, and the same clear definition of the head aura is then present from earliest times. At this period—usually around seven—the chakras change. At birth they are to be seen as shallow depressions on the surface of the aura, with a thin channel like a stalk running back to the etheric spinal cord. Gradually, however, they deepen, and at the same time come forward beyond the surface of the etheric so that they are like cornucopias or nasturtium flowers growing from the spine, and they develop a fine mesh of etheric energies like a membrane, over the open end. This membrane or web has a special function, in that it filters the impacts from the psychic world and limits what enters physical consciousness. In this way it not only shuts out invasion from the objective physical world but also from the personal unconscious or subjective psychic world of the individual himself. Jung says that insanity is "invasion from the collective", and all psychologists agree that the

insane regress—at least in one side of themselves—towards childhood. This is precisely so from the standpoint of the etheric. If serious damage occurs to the etheric, and especially to the chakras, the individual is reduced to the defenceless state he was in as an infant, and loses his adult grip on objective reality.

If development is normal and has taken place under good conditions, about the age of seven the child enters into possession of a fully formed, if not fully developed, etheric organism in which all the levels of energy will be functioning basically in the way they will function for the rest of its life. Once more the balance between each level will, in health, depend upon individual temperament. In morbid cases this basic balance may be more conspicuous by its absence than its presence. But if the child has been well handled from birth, this means that the incarnating individual has brought his own lack of balance with him, and his basic instability is not the fault of present environment. On the other hand, a potentially stable child may well become unbalanced by shocks and mishandling; but taking a long view of this, it is clear that the shocks would not occur except as part of its individual karmic pattern.

The future development of the child, his ability to learn and to concentrate, to come to grips with life as it is, all depend primarily upon the integrity and type of the etheric field he now has. It is, and we cannot repeat it too often, the bridge mechanism both between himself and the material world (because it is Atma in space-time extension), and between his personality and his spiritual Self.

6

The Second Phase: Infancy to Adolescence

It was said by Ignatius Loyola, and reiterated from an entirely different standpoint by modern psychologists, that the foundation of the personality is laid between the age of five to seven. In the foregoing chapter the same was made apparent in terms of vital energy in the physical etheric field. In the first years it is as if a selection took place from the many factors and potentialities of the child. The incoming individual, seen as a whole, is rich in such potentialities. But in a given span of life only a certain number of them can be brought into activity and worked out. The rest remain more or less latent, and in psychological language, stay in the deepest unconscious of the one concerned.

Only the germs of future possibilities show in the first phase of life. They form complex patterns which depend both on the physique built at the earth level and on the response of the psyche to the experiences which come to the young child. For the relationship of the child to its body is like that of a driver to his car. A good driver with a faulty car will move erratically along the road of life; so will a bad driver with a good car. But a good driver with a good car will be able to make his journey successfully. The matter is further complicated by the fact that the car—the body—is itself growing and developing. Most people, moreover, are mediocre drivers, even if they have a fine physique. Human beings are in general only learners, and are far from making the best of both their potentialities and of the vehicle through which these can be expressed. Hence, every human being who has not yet reached perfection has difficulties and contradictions in himself and in his life, which affect the etheric field.

Interplay between subjective self and objective environ-

ment is a constant factor in the development of conscious-ness. But at the end of this first phase of physical incarnation and growth it is as if the mind or soul had become anchored, rooted in a particular way to the soil of the body. The mind is conditioned, probably for life, by these early years, however much this conditioning may be modified by positive and therapeutic effort at a later age. Race, nationality, heredity, lie at the bottom of the pattern; experiences of all kinds, including those of health and disease, and both those of a physical and of a psychic order, form the next layer. The aggregate leads to certain mental reaction patterns which remain the basis of the personality for the rest of this span of life, however much they may elaborate themselves as time goes on and the field of individual activity spreads.

The psychologist recognizes that other patterns may be-come superimposed on the base, so that a negative overlies and hides a positive, or vice versa; or that distorted growth may result in morbid forms of behavior and thought. But in all cases neurosis rests on the foundation laid in early years, as well as on failure to develop that foundation successfully towards its teleological consummation. If this is understood we shall see that, at every stage of human experience, both the physical and the mental need to be at one with the spiritual, the Atmic, the will. The active factor is the mind, *Manas*, in its dual aspect, pivoting on its own central fourth, the *Antahkarana* of *The Secret Doctrine*. This mental fourth is in fact the dynamic center from which man lives, in both directions at once, up towards the spiritual, down towards the physical. Just as the spiritual contains the whole of man's being, including the physical, so does the physical etheric

It is at a critical moment, between the first and second phases, that this middle mental center becomes active in the personal field, bringing with it the powers we speak of —whether as theosophists or as philosophers on Bergsonian lines—as Monadic. For the Monad is no distant, remote thing, it is the power of individuality in all its forms both active and latent, and is present here and now, on the earth and in the physical body. We know only the outermost fringes

of what this individuality is. The personal, psychological *ego*, and even the other aspect of it, usually spoken of as *Ego* with a capital E, or *Self*, probably only represent a fragment of true, monadic individuality. Nevertheless, all knowledge of *ego* is essentially monadic, hence of spiritual origin and nature.

Psychological findings largely agree with the traditions of occultism on the fact that the child changes into a self-conscious individual at the threshold of the second stage, somewhere between five and seven. What the psychologist does not allow for, however, is not only that there are many exceptions to the general rule, but also that the mental age of the group to which he belongs also varies. Not only is the individual both unique and growing, but collective humanity itself is growing. So, whether one considers a Hottentot, a European or a Chinese, it is probable that the average person of five hundred years ago in any of these races was less mature than the average of today in the same race; and equally, that the child five hundred years in the future will be on the whole more sophisticated than the corresponding one today. In any case, the general principle can be laid down that there is a stage at which something emerges from the subjective realm, from within the child, and becomes projected across the etheric bridge into the objective world. That is, latent factors, already spoken of, now become active in the developing life pattern of the personality whose foundation is by now laid. The development is now largely emotional, despite the intellectual element represented in school lessons and the like. And, as it is concerned principally with the personal aspect of the individual, it can be said that school life represents a recapitulation of past stages of experience in evolution rather than the breaking of altogether new ground.

The imaginative and dramatic capacities of the mind awaken. The child begins to create his own characters and images according to his basic temperament. Hitherto he has largely copied others. Whatever he himself has initiated was very primitive, while his learning was through imitation and identification. The small girl helping mother to dust, the

little boy in front of the fire with his hands in his pockets like daddy, are identifying themselves with others, and learning as they do so. But now, the princess and the Indian chief and other symbolic figures emerge from within the individual mind and become personalities, created according to the image of the subjective mental needs in the child. They are not merely copies of outside things and people. Analysis proves that these creations are primarily of emotional value, inspired by desire. That is, new levels of energy are brought into the physical field. They represent spiritual, teleological urges reaching the physical level through desire and wishful thinking, therefore they are strongly colored by emotional factors. It may be said that these imaginative creations represent the blossoming of the emotional nature under the rays of the spiritual sun. The expression itself may not seem spiritual to the adult mind—as when a small boy becomes a pirate or a gangster, but it is a necessary stage in the spiritual development of the incarnated individual. Hence any attempt to bypass it in the name of higher morality may do harm to the development of personality and invite illness, if not disaster. J. A. Hadfield has said that if a child of six or seven is faced with a tempting dish of sweets and is too honest to help himself to them when there is nobody to restrain him it may well turn out to be too great a moral strain for his years.

In short, during the period between roughly seven and maturity, the child is and should be, under the influence of his desire nature and of the more material aspects of his mind. It is from these levels that he derives his psychological energy, and his etheric field is filled with those energies which correspond to these levels of his being. True, much intellectual work is done as time goes on, but the basis of this is acquisitive learning from others—rather than creative, however important the creative side may be. Therefore it is the proper age for the advancement of the personal self, with the emotional nature and its wish for success and personal fulfilment. It is only later, and gradually, that abstract and

idealistic motives become more prominent than personal ends.

This is the age when two main patterns of mental life, and especially of fantasy, emerge. One remains largely subjective and in-turned, the other reaches out into its environment. One child dreams quietly to itself, the other acts its fantasies out with vigor. In other words, we have the manifestation of the introvert or extrovert temperaments.

In terms of the vital field, we have an increase of the subtler aspects of the emotional and instinctive energies. The whole etheric organism becomes more elaborately and consciously responsive both to outer and inner stimuli. The introvert, however, tends to withdraw from the outside world and its inevitable unpleasantnesses. If he does this to excess he is apt to fail in the necessary vital exchange which should take place between himself and the earth on which he lives. His vital resources dwindle at the expense of his subjective life. On the other hand, excessive extraversion may give vigorous physical health at the cost of shallowness at the psychological level.

The chakras also show progressive change. But during the earlier period of this second stage the solar plexus center is the principal gate through which the emotional—not the intellectual—life expresses itself. It is stimulated from within by the child's personal selfhood—the psychological ego which is trying to assert itself in the world through feeling. *Me, my* daddy, *I* did, and *I* can: the first person singular predominates and fills the child's life. It has not yet reached the point where relationship between *me* and other *me's* comes into the field, as it does when intellect begins to overshadow simple feeling. The early years are energized primarily by feeling, and this increases the sensitivity of the solar plexus, which is often uncontrollably responsive both to external and unconscious internal stimuli; whence the fears and tendency to emotional tantrums at this age.

As the ego becomes established the tenacity with which the child holds on to his own possessions relaxes, and the etheric

field becomes relatively stable. But at first his desire to possess or to hold on to things and people makes him project outward the subtler parts of his etheric (corresponding to emotion) and wrap them round the object, much as an amoeba flows round the food particles it requires. Hence, roughly to snatch an object away from a child is to hurt it, because the etheric behaves as though it has suddenly been wrenched or twisted. Similarly, the departure of a person to whom the child is literally as well as metaphorically attached, can cause injury and shock, because in this case the etheric link is suddenly pulled apart. It is unrecognized things of this kind which account for the violent reaction, particularly of a sensitive child, to seemingly mild and unimportant events. The reaction is all out of proportion to the size of the occurrence itself. In psychological terms, one would say that it was caused by the degree to which the child's fantasy and emotional life was wrapped round the cork, the empty tin, or the piece of dirty rag which was being taken away. As a small child projects its thought and feeling towards a special toy or other physical object, so does he etherically project something of himself around it, so that if the object is roughly taken away he is literally etherically hurt.

It should be made clear at this point that the stages of development described in these chapters are only predominantly physical or emotional, etc. It is obvious that no single aspect of personality fills the whole field, but that one overlaps the other all the time. Nevertheless, the principle holds, that the prime motive at each stage is first physical sensation, then emotion and instinct, and later, intellect. In the etheric field, therefore, the main life comes from vital energies corresponding to the predominant psychological level. It is as if a series of tidal waves succeeded one another in this, one dying out as another mounts. This is particularly obvious in the relatively short phases of early life. But the same rule holds true all through, though the waves become longer and less sharply defined as life goes on.

7

The Third Phase: Adolescence to Manhood

Before modern science reduced adolescence to the results of a change in the endocrine system it was said by poets and romantically-minded people to be a period of spring-like burgeoning, of dreams and sighs, of the miracle of first love. To more prosaic people it is a time when their children are apt to become moody, introspective, secretive and unpredictable—and sometimes very trying. In fact, from different angles, both the scientist and the one who is concerned with the moods of the adolescent are right, for it is a time of major re-adjustment at both the psychic and the physical levels.

It seems probable that the first movement is actually somewhere in the nonphysical aspects of the individual. This directly affects the etheric vital field, and, in turn, the physical organism is brought into relation with what has already begun at less obvious levels. Psychologically, the child is now at a stage where he recapitulates the phases he has gone through since birth, but with a difference. He began by feeling his way into his body, becoming accustomed to physical sensation. This was succeeded by a stage of emotional adjustment, during which he was still psychically wide open to the world, his chakras and his etheric field in general being unguarded and defenseless. Then he discovered self, and with it entered on the next stage, where intellect became paramount. But all this he did within himself, with himself at the center of his world. He now starts afresh, but with a sense of growing relationship to others, to the surrounding world. "I" does not exist alone, its welfare depends on proper adjustment to "not-I"—the age of Adlerian rather than Freudian psychology.

The etheric field is profoundly affected. For new spiritual energies—some belonging to the first three of the sevenfold group—come into play. It is not surprising that their prime impact should be in the head, where their point of focus is in the region of the third ventricle to the brain. For it is from the pituitary gland that the whole process of physical adolescence is unchained, affecting principally the gonads and bringing about puberty, but also, directly or indirectly, all the other members of the endocrine system.

These in turn interlock with a change of etheric structure. Sometimes the etheric field loses its tension, sometimes it tightens; whichever it does, depends on the temperament of the individual.

Naturally, what with the psychic and the physical changes, the chakras are also disturbed, and remain so until the new pattern of both mind and body is established and stabilized. It would not be easy to give any brief description in general terms of just how they change, as this is so individual. But it can be said that during the period corresponding to most rapid physical growth they are apt to be thrown out of balance, to become unstable and over reactive and, to some extent, vulnerable in the same way as are those of a very small child. This is due to the complex nature of these centers, containing, as they do, a compound pattern of various forms and levels of vital energy. And at this time of life new currents, both from the subtler, psycho-spiritual levels and others from the chemical, come into play and have to become readjusted around the central fourth before poise and stability are regained.

Ideally speaking, as adolescence reaches its end, all the centers become readjusted and balanced, as do the endocrine glands, so that the whole psycho-physiological system is once again integrated and healthy. But whether this balance is reached depends on an aggregation of factors, both physical and psychological.

Leaving the former aside, since such things as the need for hygiene, proper food, etc., are well-known, the rest depends

very much on psychological forces. And if an individual is not properly adjusted in this sphere, though his body may grow into that of a healthy adult, his subtler mechanism will tend to be faulty, in that the chakras—the organs of psychic communication—do not gain a proper and equal degree of maturity. The result may be that one has a person physically mature but emotionally childish, with a labile solar plexus, which in turn unbalances the whole system in one way or another. This is why one may have an over intellectual adult. who is nevertheless emotionally uncontrolled and receptively psychic in a mediumistic way, behind the facade of a hard, scientific outlook: too hard and scientific, indeed, to be as genuine or as sound as he believes it to be. In this sense one finds that there are some people who remain partly adolescent all their days, for only positive work on themselves and on their emotional nature can, after this, come to the rescue and produce a balance hitherto lacking between their earthy and their spiritual natures.

In general, entry into adult life is a great factor in steadying the individual. The end of formal education, the fact that many leave the parental home and take on responsibility for themselves, fall in love (disturbing as this is at the time), marriage, parenthood, civic responsibility and all the other things which make a young man or woman turn outward and face life, are potent factors in bringing to maturity the powers which have begun to manifest during adolescence. This means that the vital field becomes an active, responsive organism through which the inner man acts and is acted on by the outside world. The young adult is at the fullest point of physical power and capacity. He is set on his life pattern, and though this will change as he settles down, it is apt to do so only on the logical tracks of the railroad on which he has now started. This is why so many crystallize into middle age, thereby storing up troubles in both physical and mental health for the next stage of life. But if the individual is self-aware and creative he will be constantly bringing new energies to bear on the pattern now set, so that it will grow

and develop indefinitely without ever reaching a stopping point until death deprives him, if only temporarily, of the opportunity to go further in the physical world.

8

Maturity and After

At the end of a number of years during which the adult should be maturing and establishing himself in the world, another change, comparable to that of puberty, takes place. This is the climacteric, well-known and clearly defined in women, less definite but just as real in men. There is no fixed age for this. It is usually later in men than women.

From the endocrine point of view this stage represents the reverse of puberty. The sexual glands become less active as time goes on, though, of course, this does not reverse the processes of puberty or mean reversion to a childish state, whether of mind or body. Nor does it follow from this that sexuality dies out as it does in animals. This may be due to the human faculty of association and memory, or it may be due to a more complex sexual pattern in human beings. Nevertheless, the climacteric represents entry into a new phase of life, both psychic and physiological. Once again the time lag between the psychic and the bodily change operates.

Normally and naturally it should show a transference of psychic energy from physical and material preoccupations to a more philosophical level. This is why so many people do their best work, their personalities blossoming, in middle age, and showing creative capacities perhaps unsuspected in earlier life. Concurrently with this, the etheric field also changes. In terms of it there should be a progressive emphasis on the finer energies at the expense of the others. The vegetative, terrene pattern tends to slow down, adjusting its tempo to that of the quieter and more harmonious life of the aging individual.

This is an ideal state and is, obviously, far from being reached by most people. It is perhaps one reason for the increase of mental and physical illness as middle and old age

are approached. For though age is bound to be a progressive weakening of the dense vital fabric, culminating in death, there is no intrinsic reason, other than psychological lack of harmony, for disease to be prevalent rather than a gradual and peaceful road towards death.

In the ideal, the change of balance towards the spiritual should result in a transformation of the vital pattern, in which catabolism rather than anabolism becomes predominant, so that the body gradually wears out. At the same time, however, poised consciousness and awareness should be redressing the balance of the whole individual, so that he becomes increasingly serene as he grows older.

How far this is from being realized is only too obvious. Many people dread old age and try to hold on to the past, both in terms of physical power and of the desire to repeat pleasant experience. They are unwilling to let go of these and to adjust to their age. Hence there is conflict and unhappiness, and these cause a new kind of disharmony in the vital field, and are almost certainly a main cause of middle-aged ill-health.

If the climacteric goes well, there is no serious and sudden change in the physical and psychic well-being of the individual. On the other hand, the unbalance associated with the endocrine change may lead to aggravation of pre-existing neurosis or to physical ill-health caused by a lack of adjustment of the various vital levels to the new phase of physical life. The etheric once again becomes uncoordinated, loses its vital continence, and the solar plexus chakra in particular behaves like a swinging door in a gusty wind.

As against this, there are a number of factors which may lead to better health. For one thing many people are better established in the material sense, their career is assured and earlier insecurity and stress disappear. For another, they may by now have found their life work and interest. And third, there are people whose physical life, with its sexual rhythm and urges, has always been a problem. The easing of this may remove a point of stress from their minds—even if it has not been positively resolved.

There is a fourth type, rarer than the others, in whom the

climacteric represents a point of resolution of the positive work they may have been doing on their character for many years. At last, it seems, things fall into place and their inner life becomes much more orderly and satisfactory than ever before. In short, if people are happier in middle age than they were earlier in life, they may well enjoy better health and find new vigor, both physical and mental.

This shows in the etheric field in better coordination, less tension, and a general resiliency of its fabric, while the energy currents themselves become stronger and more harmonious. The solar plexus chakra especially becomes steadier and less apt to be upset by emotional storms.

Much, therefore, depends on the frame of mind with which middle and old age are approached. If seen as disaster, a disaster it will be. If seen as a natural and progressive state it can be a time of increasing happiness and depth of perception which makes life—despite diminishing physical power—a thing of ever-growing interest and richer experience.

9

The Act of Dying

The obvious and only certain fact about death is that the body
ceases to function as an integrated whole. It gradually re-
solves itself into lower and yet lower biological, and ultimately chemical, levels. Of the other aspect of death, concerned with the fate of the individual inhabiting the body, it
must frankly be said that one can only speculate, even if one
accepts the basic principle of the immortality of the spirit.
Details of what happens "on the other side" are obscure; and
every description of posthumous life is more or less colored by
wishful thinking. Moreover, such descriptions are inevitably
couched in language related to physical happenings.

From the point of view of the etheric field, bodily death
represents a final cleavage between the psycho-spiritual and
the chemical levels of the vital organism. That is, a process
occurs which is somewhat similar to what takes place in sleep
or any other form of physical unconsciousness, but it is irreversible. The middle, or fourth, layer is not only temporarily inhibited, it is actually and finally broken up. The result is
like taking the keystone out of an arch: there is no longer any
bridge between one side and the other, and each half of the
structure tends to crumble and resolve into its elements.

Clairvoyantly, the Biblical analogy of the "silver cord" is
good. For at the moment of death, it is as if a luminous ray
flashed out through the top of the head (actually, the crown
chakra), after which a more or less rapid fading of bodily
activity ensues. The heart may go on beating for a few mi-
nutes, the muscles remain responsive to electrical stimuli,
and so on. But step by step these functions cease, together
with metabolic processes, and the body stiffens until it is
taken over by bacterial decomposition.

It seems as if what takes place is the reverse of what happens at the beginning of incarnation, but it is simpler as far as the devic life is concerned. For whereas there always appears to be angelic supervision of the moment of death—in Christian language, Azrael is said to be the Angel of Death—the subsequent disintegration does not require the same intelligent, constructive activity as in the beginning, but is left to simple elemental forces. In Chapter Three, the image was given of a spinning golden nucleus entering a field prepared by devic-elemental agents, after which active gestation proceeds. Here we have the withdrawal of this nucleus prior to the dissipation of the material originally gathered together, and subsequently held in proper form round its focus.

At this point, once more, anything said must be looked upon as tentative, and as the result of what empirical observation is possible. For death contains a mystery which man has not fathomed except in a subjective and entirely personal way. We know nothing of life after death except from purely individual accounts, derived from such subjective experience; and those, even if true, have to be expressed in the only language available, which is formed around the observation of physical events. And it is doubtful whether the afterworld is as much like the physical as these descriptions suggest.

It seems as if the indwelling spirit, manifest as soul in psychic sphere, and hitherto inhabiting the dense body in the physical, gradually retires into its own world. That is, after losing its dense anchorage, a process of resolution takes place, comparable to that in the physical organism, but being on the other side of the fourth, its movement is away from the dense physical and towards the spiritual. Of the later stages—those in the pure psychic world—we cannot speak. But it appears as if, after physical death, the psychic vital levels of the etheric organism retain their coherence for a time. This is largely due to mental habit. During physical life the mind usually becomes heavily identified with the body image reaching it through the physical brain. This induces in

the mind an impression that it is only through the body that it is truly conscious. True, this is a matter of degree, and depends on how much the individual is aware of himself apart from this body, at the psychic or astro-mental level. But where the person is strongly attached to physical experience and sensation, the persistence of the body image is strong, and may last for a long time after physical death. This holds together the subtler part of the old etheric field which, though no longer tied to the heavy physical body, keeps the shape to which it has been accustomed and follows the contours of the mental image.

It is an interesting point that an old person strongly attached to a particular environment and routine will, if seen clairvoyantly after death, continue to appear in the same aged form. But a more vital and interiorly dynamic individual may, perhaps because he is so much relieved at being free of the impediment of his body, quickly resume the aspects of youth. In any case, as time goes on, the image tends to fade. This is why apparitions, on the whole, tend to be commonest soon after death. The longer the time which has passed since death, the rarer they become—and, indeed, many ghosts belong to comparatively recent history. It is not often that Greek warriors or Roman senators are said to haunt a place. Far more often they date from only a few decades or years back. As against this, it is often some time after a loved relative has died that those left behind get an inner sense of contact with him. This may be partly accounted for by recovery from shock on the part of the living one, but it may also be that the dead has become freer from his old attachments and so more able to make positive contact from within with those who are still thinking of him.

It must be made clear that vision of a dead person is not the same thing as psychometrizing the past of a place. There are innumerable records of visions among people visiting Egyptian temples and other places of great antiquity. But it is most likely that these are based on the memory record of the place rather than on the persistence of any actual person or group of people in that place. Moreover, one must remember

too that if one sees a dead relative his appearance may be less of himself as he actually is, than strongly conditioned by the mental habit of the percipient in thinking of him in a certain appearance. So that it may be we who give him a certain resemblance to his late physical form rather than that he himself is still in that form.

In writing this we are well aware that we are making generalizations which can be offset in all directions by many individual examples. Nevertheless, the main principle seems to hold good and to explain the majority of cases.

At the same time, a number of interesting points arise. For when a dead person is seen he appears only in the guise of his physical body and has no visible aura. In theory, however, he should be mainly aura, with little physical form. Why does this not work out? Possibly because most people are unused to thinking in terms of an aura, and hence themselves supply only the image of a physical body but do not naturally think of an aura around it. But in any case it seems as if it were a matter of perception and the language of perception: a complex matter which can only be understood if we first consider the question of the relation between mind as the observer and the physical field which it observes.

10

Health and Disease

Physical health depends on a proper balance and integration of the many energy streams in the etheric or vital body.

The terrene energies correspond to the dense physical, hence continuity of tissue is essential to their proper flow. Broken bones, cut nerves and other physical injuries obstruct or prevent their function. Equally, anything which interferes with the energy flow may lead to tissue necrosis and to trophic injuries. Starvation, general or local, lack of essential ingredients in food, destructive ray therapy, such as x-ray or radium emanation, may cause breakdown of physical tissue by breaking up the pattern of the etheric field at the terrene level.

The subtler forces affect *function* in the body. Themselves associated with psychic and mental levels, they play primarily into the sympathetic and endocrine systems through the chakras. They are also associated with physical consciousness. They circulate through the whole body but they appear to be connected with the physical nervous system and its ganglia, as also with endocrine function.

A first assessment would suggest that the terrene forces work mainly through the sacral parasympathetic plexus and the sacral (*muladhara*) chakra; certain others act through the solar plexus and the dorsal sympathetic chain; while the finest enter through the head centers and play not only through the cortical levels in connection with conscious activity but also through the superior parasympathetic, or vagal, system at *sub*conscious levels (the prefix *sub* meaning that aspect of the *un*conscious as a whole).

The interplay of the forces between the sacral parasympathetic and the sympathetic is also subconscious, and governs

the metabolic processes of the body. The vagal sympathetic pattern is, though linked to conscious behavior, modified by instinctive, unconscious factors arising from the sympathetic system.

In practice, it is very difficult to say where each level of coordinated function begins and ends. For movement anywhere in the etheric field requires adjustment of the whole. Conscious action, involving the use of the muscles, leads to a metabolic reaction to supply the fuel needed by these muscles; while a deep disturbance due to nutrition may reflect itself, as a secondary event, in strangeness of consciousness and behavior. Thus, the spiritual orientation of a person has a direct bearing on his physical health, while physical illness affects, if not strictly speaking his mind, his consciousness and behavior at the physical level. Moreover, the psychic levels corresponding to the middle period of mental development, and corresponding to the older evolutionary levels of the nervous system—from sympathetic to thalamic—forms the bridge between the two and is itself of great importance, being the realm in which the psyche touches the physical, and hence is the starting point of functional or psychosomatic disease.

The importance of this middle realm is intuitively realized today as holding the key to proper alignment throughout the individual. The demand for self-awareness and for diminishing the field of unconscious, primitive motivation and its sway over the conscious field of willed, or solar, behavior governed by free choice, is an expression of this. Groddeck shows how psychic disgruntlement is a prime cause in vegetative, functional disease, leading to the psychosomatic type of trouble and eventually to actual organic tissue change. Jung shows how unconscious, instinctive, and hence archaic, factors can stand between man and spiritual self-realization. Both show that disease is due to imbalance somewhere in the total field, producing further imbalance in the rest of it.

This principle is also in line with ancient Hindu and Chinese medicine, though in the latter only the dual polarity of Yin and Yang is mentioned. Yet there can be no poles

without a field between them. Whether one tackles disease from the point of view of opposite poles (thus implying a third and intermediate factor), or from that of the field (which can only exist if there are poles from which it arises) is comparatively unimportant. What is important, however, is that disease should not be thought of as exclusively rooted in any single component of the threefold man.

Health can therefore be defined as integration of spirit, soul or psyche and body. Or, in terms of the vital field, of solar and terrene energies. But a further factor has to be taken into consideration, which is time. For a person may be—and, in fact, usually is—fully integrated only for a moment. After this, the balance of forces represented by that integration is upset by the fact that the moment of time has passed and that what was right and fully valid at that moment is no longer so in the next. Evolution demands constant movement and progress. Hence, the living entity has to undergo perpetual readjustment and rebalancing if it is to remain healthy. And the focus of this readjustment is essentially in the mind, where there is a tendency for the earth-turned aspects to contend against the forces of progress and of increasing consciousness by trying to settle down into mental and emotional grooves. If this inertia reflects into the vital etheric field it too fails to keep pace with the passage of time, and illness results.

In spite of this emphasis on the singleness of man and of the threefold vital field, a further generalization can be made in saying that where the main point of stress is between the intermediate and the terrene forces, the result is psychosomatic, then somatic illness. If, on the other hand, the prime stress is between this and the solar, the result is mental disease: psychoneurosis and possible psychosis.

All types of disease can be diagnosed through the etheric field if sufficient fine discrimination is possible on the part of the observer. Moreover, disturbance of this field often shows for some time before any overt manifestation of illness appears. Thus a tendency to malignant disease may be seen before the usual medical methods are able to diagnose even a precancerous state, let alone an actual local growth. In other

cases, general disorganization of the etheric occurs for some days before the onset of an acute and transitory disease such as a fever, or for much longer during the time before a chronic or subacute specific illness sets in.

A general classification seems to be possible—and this too is in line with Chinese medicine—between diseases where there is excess of vitality and activity where tissue tends to burn up, and those where there is too little, and, consequently, inertia and tissue lethargy. Tuberculosis, for instance, is a consuming illness, while arthritis is one of stagnation and congestion. In endocrine diseases the difference is particularly obvious in its results at the physical level. Myxedema and other forms of underactivity of the thyroid can, for instance, be set against Graves' disease and toxic goitre in general. In mental diseases, too, the opposites of agitation and passivity, of mania and depression, of catatonia and the violent outbursts of schizophrenics, are equally obvious.

We have also to think of the quantitative proportions of the energies involved. This has to take into account the qualitative activity of these energies, whatever their quantity. Too much terrene energy may, for instance, lead to congestion and stasis if these are passive, to hypertrophy if they are active. Add to this excess of active solar energy and further complications may occur, such as the hypertrophy being benign or malignant. Excess of solar activity over terrene, however, may lead to consuming diseases such as tuberculosis, already mentioned, Graves' disease or diabetes. All-round deficiency may, however, result simply in impoverishment of the whole etheric field, so that (a) actual vitality leaks out of the terrene structure, thereby making things worse than ever, and (b) deficiency diseases occur, with lack of maintenance of physical tissue: anemia, skin troubles, trophic ulcers, etc. It is also in such conditions that external factors such as bacteria, viruses, etc., find easy entry into the system and cause their characteristic disease syndromes. Moreover, the thinness of the etheric structure leads to exaggerated reactions and to allergic conditions of psychogenic origin.

This not being a book on medicine, only a few generali-

zations such as these can be given. The problem, however, is highly complex; and when one comes to diseases like asthma one is faced with a complex imbalance as between several orders of energy, some representing the psychological factor in this complaint, others the physical and allergic component.

Where mental disease is concerned, the primary seat of the trouble appears to be between the psychic and spiritual aspects of man, whatever secondary efforts there may be at the bodily level junction, for the whole etheric field is apt to be involved.* But while physical illness can readily be linked with known anatomical structures and physiological functions in the dense body, mental disease involves an etheric anatomy quite unknown to Western science, and one not necessarily reproduced in physical structure. Much has been learned about mental illness, but still more remains obscure. In fact, psychiatrists of vision, like Adolf Meyer, recognizing this, take up the attitude that beyond a certain point there is mystery and that neurology will not explain it. Jung, on the other hand, openly states that the mind is and must always remain mysterious, since the spiritual is ever beyond the reach of intellectual and scientific apprehension. Study of the etheric carries neurology and psychiatry a step further when, as in the East, it is realized that there are channels and currents of energy—*nadis, Sushumna, Kundalini* and the like—the very existence of which is unsuspected by ordinary science, and detailed knowledge of which involves an immense amount of study and meditation. Moreover, such study would be unwise except under expert guidance. For the most part, these forces are best left to take care of themselves and to adjust themselves automatically to the changing consciousness of the mind working at its own level. Many disasters result from such practices as "sitting for development" or *hatha yoga* and *pranayama* exercises, and these may be attributed to premature or unwise interference with these forces

---

* Recent medical research points to chemical-physical causes for some forms of mental illness, though by no means can this be interpreted to mean that it would be the only cause nor the reason for the majority of cases.

or the channels in which they flow.

In mental illness the basic principle is particularly apparent that all disease and, in fact, all discomfort, even that which appears to come from external causes, is due to maladjustment to spiritual urges. Man should live anchored between sun and earth. Therefore it is clear that for a proper balance to be achieved there must be equality between the poles, and consequently that the psychic field between them must be in a state of poise, not unduly pulled in one direction or the other.

All three aspects of the triple field are important; the terrene because it provides the basic structure through which physical consciousness plays. This base may be firm and stable, or it may be weak, either through ill health, drugs, or from hereditary causes. Moreover, it needs to be linked both firmly and pliably with the intermediate psychic side, so that there is in it an elastic yet resilient joint mechanism for the spiritual life. Heredity does not itself cause mental disease. But as is well-known, there are cases where there may be a strong earthy physique but the link with the psyche is faulty and facilitates, without causing, mental illness when circumstances become strenuous and cannot be born without damage. That is, when conflict either between the thinking and feeling parts of the mind, or within the joint thinking-feeling organism occurs, this is apt to injure the weak psycho-physical junction and neurosis or insanity become manifest. Inevitably, too, this means that in the background of the manifest disease there is a lack of spiritual harmony which reflects into the terrene field, which is identical with spirit but extended in space-time.

The chakras, that part of the psychic anatomy, are always involved in mental disease. These centers are governed from within, by the subtle and complex energies of the interior man—energies comparable to those which keep the physical sense organs healthy and functional. It is worth mentioning at this point that the association of the chakras with physical organs—heart, spleen, etc.—is only approximate. The *muladhara*, for instance, said to be at the base of the spine, is

in the region of the sacrum, and well below the extremity of the spinal cord, which terminates at the lower end of the second lumbar vertebra, several inches above the sacrum. Other discrepancies of similar order can be found in linking centers with physical structures, but the point remains, that the inner, narrower end of the chakras is actually in the etheric counterpart of the spinal cord or brain—this counterpart extending beyond the confines of the physical nervous structure both above the head and below the end of the cord, in much the same way as the etheric aura extends beyond the outline of the physical body.

Physical stress may injure the dense body. Similarly, psychological stress may injure the vital aspects of the etheric, and particularly the chakras. The function of these is manifold, but they are, as has been said, the essential link between physical consciousness and the various levels of the psychic and spiritual worlds. One aspect of them, moreover, and one which concerns us deeply in connection with mental disease is that they are the main foci for the devic-elemental life of various orders. It has been said, in fact, that the human chakra is actually the body through which the devas partake in the physical life of the incarnate human being. If the chakra is damaged, either the devic life becomes cut off, or it overwhelms the individual and is out of control. In this way, the various psychopathic syndromes can be linked with different chakras or groups of chakras, and with the particular kind of devic and elemental life to which they correspond. It is worth noting, also that in general terms, the psychologists' theories as to the mechanisms of these syndromes correspond to what is known of the chakras involved. Over-anxiety, for instance, and all that goes with it, produces cramping and distortion of the solar plexus center. This, in turn, reacts on the denser etheric levels and eventually affects physical function. Then arises obscure digestive troubles, with pain, colic and sickness, irregular heart beat, etc. Then, when the matter goes beyond the functional, psychosomatic stage, ulceration and even malignancy may follow.

Many cases, however, remain in the psychic field only. In

schizophrenia, for instance, anatomists and physiologists look in vain for physical changes. The disease remains at the subtler etheric levels, where the head aura appears to be cleft, and the currents of vital energy which should circulate and interweave over the top of the head to give a smooth outline to the aura turn back on themselves, as a swift river can be split into divergent streams by a rock. This rock is always a complex, tight knot of intense feeling material, compressed and telescoped into a small space by thought running in a narrow pattern. In certain cases the compression goes on until an explosion occurs and we have the outbursts of violence typical in catatonia. In other cases, the paranoid variety, the tight compression is absent but there is still an isolated complex in the split, in which a repetitive chain of ideas goes round and round like a goldfish in a bowl.

The schizoid psychological temperament is notably creative, whether it be psychotic and his aura split as described, or not. Yet even the psychotic schizophrenic is at times an artist of true merit—like van Gogh—while others create monstrosities. In both of these the auric movement seems to be the same. But what we have called the rock is perhaps more in the nature of a womb space into which energies from both sides of the split can play. It is as if each side represented either masculine or feminine energies which should normally mingle, but which have become divided. They now fertilize the womb and the result is creation. But whether this be of a monster, or a work of art will depend on the type and level of the energies entering the creative field. If they come principally from spiritual sources the result will be of one kind; if from terrene levels, of another. In our galleries of modern art there are a number of pictures and sculptures which are blatantly schizophrenic. Some, like van Gogh's, are beautiful and uplifting, while others, perhaps equally brilliant in execution and technique, are imbued with a kind of psychic undertow showing that they are the product of an unhealthy psyche in which the terrene forces are exaggerated.

The *ajna* (brow) and solar plexus chakras appear to be the

principal ones involved in schizophrenia, with subsidiary effects elsewhere. The disease appears to be the result of a profound and continuous refusal of the individual to follow his spiritual path, his *dharma,* through a number of incarnations. In such cases there comes a time when the conflict between spirit and personal psyche is so acute that breakdown of the etheric mechanism—perhaps made easier by a weak heredity—occurs. The individual is, literally, dragged in two by the conflict, and the split—whether we think of this in terms of psychology or of the etheric aura—is held open by the resistance of the psyche to the laws of its true being. This conflict, taking on an objective form in the etheric field, and having acquired an automatic life of its own, forms the wedge in the split, and so remains until eventually liquidated and resolved by the individual as a result of his own endeavors to redeem himself.

Owing to the breakdown of the etheric mechanism in these cases, true dementia may set in, with progressive deterioration of the whole personality, and the primitive elemental life of the psychic organism gradually takes control, ousting the last remnants of control by the will of the individual. The end result, in such cases, is the type sometimes to be seen in mental hospitals, where the victim behaves in an entirely automatic fashion, scarcely retaining the character of a human being. In fact, he resembles, though in a living body, the kind of automatic ghost so often found in haunted houses, which we described in an earlier chapter.

Manic-depressive psychosis, or cyclothymia, has two distinct phases, representing extremes of the same condition. They are coupled together because it happens that a depressed person may swing over to acute mania and back again to depression in alternating periods. It is true, of course, that many cases do not go so far, and a manic may settle down to a comparatively normal state between attacks, or another come out of depression without going into a state of exaggerated hilarity. The exact reason for this is not easy to determine, despite much research, but what happens is that the emotions of the victim get out of hand and behave like rising

or falling water. He may know intellectually what is taking place, but mind and will have no control over the situation. Indeed, part of the work of psychiatrists in dealing with such cases is to try and educate the patient to recognize the early symptoms of an attack and to place himself voluntarily under treatment before things go too far. From the psychic view point it is once again the elemental-devic life which has taken control though, in these cases, the intellectual aspect is divorced from that of feeling and not as in schizophrenia where mind and feeling together are divided within themselves.

In depression the etheric aura loses its vitality and becomes grey and foggy. As a result, feeling about external objects and people is numbed and all that is left is a sense of imprisonment within one's own grey world. In due time, in most cases, the tide returns and the depression lifts until the next cycle repeats the process. In mania the exact reverse occurs and vitality is excessive, perceptions acute, and reactions exaggerated. Then, once again, the flood waters ebb and there is a return to normal. There are no statistics relating these cycles to the phases of the moon; and, indeed, attacks of mania or depression often last for weeks or months. Yet the popular term lunatic might be found to be true if it were realized that the trouble here is in the middle or lunar aspects of the psychic field.

In paranoia—persecution mania, or delusions of grandeur not associated with syphilis or other physical disease—the patient is entirely normal until certain subjects are broached, when a system of ideas becomes active, which is not open to argument or common sense. The nature of the trouble is traceable to psychological causes, but the reason for the breakdown which makes the paranoid thought system inaccessible seems to lie first in a cleavage in the mind of the victim. In it frustrated power plays a major part, leading to a sense of guilt and, by compensation for this guilt, of superiority to others. Not unexpectedly, as paranoid ideas are based on perverse reasoning, the main change is about the head aura, in which anything which starts the thought system into

activity produces a repetitive series of movements which resemble those scenes occurring in ancient clocks when they strike the hour. These strong, if automatic, thoughts push the etheric aura out into balloon-like shapes, always in the same sequence, until, as it were, the clock runs down and everything is quiet until the next time. Here, too, an emotional stimulus touches off the process and the elemental life, dissociated from and out of control of the will, is the dynamic factor. The *ajna* chakra, which is concerned with perceptivity, is the one mainly involved and its disorganization accounts for the falsity of the paranoiac's assessment of the meaning of events.

Obsessional and compulsive neuroses are similar to paranoia in that an idea becomes isolated from the context of the rest of the mind and acquires a life of its own. The isolated idea becomes exaggerated and a whole system—of thought in the case of paranoia, but of action in these cases—is set in motion by a certain stimulus. Thus the idea of possible contamination by germs makes the compulsive person wash, not once but perhaps twenty times on end, before he can rest. Then, perhaps, something happens to suggest once more that the person is unclean, and a whole ritual of ablutions has once more to be undergone from beginning to end. The difference between this and paranoia is that the latter projects his ideas on to his environment: other people persecute him, he says, not facing the fact that it is he who blames himself. In compulsion and obsession the whole system is self-contained and within a very narrow space. Moreover, the thoughts behind the ritual acts refer to physical things, "I am dirty, I must be clean", "I must not walk on the cracks in the pavement, or else . . . ", "I must never walk under a ladder or Nemesis will overtake me", and so on. Even excessive tidiness—useful in an office, but often making life difficult outside it—can be of the nature of this form of neurosis.

In the etheric field the disease is visible in the head aura, where a similar repetitive pattern to that of paranoia can be seen. But whereas paranoia is due to conflict in the emotional and mental aspect, this disease is due to frustration of simple

but powerful earthy instinctive drives such as sex or appetite
for food or material possessions. The result is that the terrene
energies become dissociatied from the mind and to some
extent autonomous. The elemental life, once more. has es-
caped from or been forced out of the control of mind and will
and tries to seek gratification and fulfilment on its own
terms. The *ajna* chakra is again profoundly involved, since
will and mind are concerned in trying to control the explosion
of physical desires, but the origin seems to lie at the opposite
end of the body, in the *muladhara* (sacral) chakra—in which
it corresponds psychologically to the analysts' view that the
obsessional syndrome belongs to the pregenital, anal-erotic
levels of the mind.

Paranoid and obsessional ideas are common in hysteria,
but the hysterical pattern is different. Hysteria is predominantly emotional, the intellectual factor being secondary.
Hence the solar plexus is the chakra mainly affected, being
either cramped and paralyzed or else wide open and defenceless. These two states often alternate, and when a crisis
occurs the center is thrown into convulsive action which
affects the whole etheric. Its balance is for the time being
destroyed and this leads to all kinds of manifestations, from
delusions and hallucinations to epileptiform fits, and to physical disabilities which do not correspond to any special cause
in the physical body, even in their anatomical distribution.

One of the aspects of hysteria is where dissociation of
personality takes place. This may show in loss of memory,
disorientation and confusion; or it may produce the sub-
stitution of one more or less complete personality for another,
as in mediumistic trance, each personality being a facet of the
mind of the victim. And one may have partial dissociation
leading to anaesthesia of a limb, or to that limb becoming
active on its own, as in automatic writing or drawing. And so
on.

In these cases the aura in general changes its quality and
tone in tune with the personality in charge of outer behavior.
If only a limb is affected there is in addition a change in the
localized part of the aura. It can also happen, as in trance or

under hypnosis, that the whole of the subtler part of the etheric is to some extent dislocated from its dense counterpart and held in a kind of static, suspended condition— the point of dislocation being the middle layer of the counter sevenfold field.

11

The Bridge of Consciousness

It was suggested in Chapter Two that there is in the etheric field a middle layer or level, the fourth of the traditional seven, which is the link between physical consciousness and the inner or psychic worlds. This is an over-simplification, and needs elaboration if we are to go more deeply into the function of the etheric field from the viewpoint of consciousness—to study that function in psychological terms. We need to examine it from three different angles:

1. Its anatomical position.
2. Its function in terms of the vital economy of the system—its physiology.
3. Its function in terms of consciousness—its psychology.

1.) The etheric is, or should be, an integrated whole. But just as in the dense body there is a concentration of certain tissues in certain parts of the organism—blood in heart and vessels, muscle in limbs, etc.—so there are areas in which one or other of the streams of etheric energy predominates. One of these is in the immediate neighborhood of the physical skin, where in many descriptions of the etheric aura, including Kilner's, a layer is noted which extends from half to one inch beyond the skin. This appears to be the place of maximum concentration of the energy patterns of this middle layer. The ribbon (as it has been called from its appearance in profile against the outline of the body) seems to be such an area of concentration of energy, and to have a particular density for reasons connected with its particular nature. This nature concerns:

2.) Its vital physiology. The central layer lies between two divisions of the physical-etheric world which, in older de-

scriptions, were described as if they were different properties, the one being called etheric, the other dense physical.

There is justification for thus speaking of four etheric layers and then placing gases, liquids, and solids beyond, and not considering them as etheric. When these descriptions were made the nature of matter was not so well-understood as today, but if one studies the two aspects of the physical world from the human angle its reasonableness becomes apparent. For the dense physical matter out of which the body is made is, in occult tradition, held not to be a principle of man himself; it is a vesture as much outside the human constitution as the clothes he puts on his body. True, the dense body is highly organized, but that does not necessarily imply that the life principle which does the organizing is *man's* life. On the contrary, the dense body is, in essence, animated by *animal* levels of life, belonging to the earlier kingdom; and it is from the animals that man has, as it were, borrowed his physical vehicle.

Further consideration of this takes us into the psychological field, of which more will be said in the next section. Its relevance here, however, is the role of the middle layer in vital physiology. For it appears to function as a reservoir of energy: a place where, under proper conditions, two main orders of vitality (prana) meet, and from being actual energy pass into a state of suspension, or latency, from which they can be recalled into actuality as the need arises. It is as if, meeting, the two streams neutralized and cancelled one another out; the energy vanishes, passes, as one might say, into another dimension, and is to all intents and purposes gone from sight. The two streams come—one from outside the system—being derived from earth, air, light, food, etc., and reach the layer from below, while the other derives from the psychic and spiritual aspects of the individual (be it animal or man) and impinge on this etheric level from above.

If the streams are equally balanced, as we have suggested, they fill the reservoir here established. But one can fill a cylinder or a balloon with gas under pressure, and release it at will. Both gas and container are under stress. Here, how-

ever, when a state of balance is reached there appears to be no stress, yet, when called upon, energy flows out precisely as if it had been under pressure inside its container. This can best be explained by two analogies. One of these is the animal liver: anabolic processes take glucose from the system, build it into glycogen and store it in the liver where it stays quietly as in a warehouse. When the body needs fuel, catabolism sets to work, reduces the glycogen once more to glucose and sends it into the blood for immediate use. The glycogen, however, is chemically stable and does not need any energy or stress to keep it as it is.

The other analogy is the ordinary electrical accumulator. This so-called because (allowing for wastage and other imperfections) if one puts into it one kilowatt of electrical energy on can at any time, by closing the circuit, draw that kilowatt out again. But till the terminals are joined the battery is electrically quite inert; it has no electrical charge comparable to that which can be put into a Leiden jar or produced by rubbing a piece of sealing wax with silk. The electricity has disappeared (actually, absorbed into chemical processes), yet it is ready to reappear instantaneously in the form of current the moment it is needed.

So in the fourth etheric layer are reserves of vitality. One may (by an unscientific analogy) say that the earth energies and the inner, psycho-spiritual energies, represent positive and negative electricity with which the accumulator is charged, and that they now become neutral electricity. Then when energy is required, for any purpose, they separate again and function as positive and negative.*

This principle seems basic, the two poles being, at root, the

---

*It is worth adding that from a psychic viewpoint the analogy of the battery is more accurate than from the scientific. For careful clairvoyant observation of the latter, not unexpectedly, shows that while the current known to science as electricity flows in one direction between the poles it is counterbalanced by another current of a subtler order flowing in the other. Thus the idea of positive and negative electricity (already to some extent accepted by science, since electrostatic charges can be either positive or negative, and each represents something actual, with similar properties) is, from the psychic angle, correct.

spiritual or atmic principle of man on the one hand, and the dense physical on the other. There is a profound correspondence between these, in that this atmic principle coincides with the etheric at the fourth level, the latter being, as it were, atma extended in space-time. Ideally, the two should be perfectly balanced, but in practice such balance is not often perfectly achieved. For the spiritual aspect of man can, for a long time, make itself felt in the physical world, and from inside the individual, only indirectly, relayed and distorted by the mind. More over, from the dense physical aspect, unbalance may result—also by the use of the mind, in its possibly erroneous choice of food, conditions of life, etc.

Then again, breathing profoundly influences vital balance. Not only is it necessary to have adequate ventilation of the lungs, but breathing also acts as a kind of pump, or heart, for the circulation of vital energy through the system. Also, the rhythm of the breathing is directly attuned to the state of mind of the individual, so that his thought processes are highly important in producing balance or otherwise of the vital field, and in determining whether or not it can hold reserves of energy.

To anyone not familiar with the effect of the breath on the etheric it would seem almost inconceivable that individual ways of breathing should make such a great difference to the texture, quality, and general vitality of the entire etheric field—to say nothing of the marked difference of appearance seen clairvoyantly. One has to remember that each person's manner of breathing is not only an automatic habit of the physical body, but that it is governed to a large extent by temperament and psychological make-up.

Anyone who is habitually anxious and frightened seldom takes an easy deep breath, but is apt to breathe unevenly and in jerks. This produces a curious irregularity in the etheric, destroying its even rhythm and creating an appearance of broken undulations, often dull grey in color. To the trained eye this indicates the fact that vital energy is uncertain, the individual probably working in spurts, then suddenly flagging.

Someone else, living under psychological strain allied to physical pressure, quickly develops the habit of rapid, shallow breathing, often using only the top of the lungs. In this case the etheric field tenses the fabric as it were, stiffens and the whole structure loses its natural pliability. In this state of tension it is impossible for it to store vitality. What there is, is used immediately. The result is loss of etheric tone and coloring, until at a point of extra strain the whole breaks down into temporary or long-term inability to carry the necessary energies for healthy living.

At the other end of the scale is the man who lives and works at his own pace, refusing to be harried or hurried. He is generally well-earthed by temperament, and in consequence his etheric field is strongly vitalized by the heavier etheric energies, and his breathing, being deep and slow, gives him an added vital stability. The appearance of such an etheric is rather like looking at a pool of quiet silvery-grey water. Its movement is slow, but it is in full correspondence with the man who creates it.

It we look about us and see the number of people who are in more or less bad health it is clear that the balance ideally required in the etheric, and particularly at the fourth layer of it, is more often than not precarious or nonexistent. The reason for this lies in:

3.) The psychological factors in human life. For man is, by his very nature, an ambiguous creature: more than an animal, less than a god, yet partly animal and also partly god. And it is because of this ambiguity that he is what he is: potentially highly creative, a dynamic force in the universe, and also a rather piteous, weak, vacillating creature, ever pulled apart between conflicting urges in himself.

This can be made clear if we consider the occult principles involved. For the field of the animal overlaps with, but does not extend as far as, the human field. Animal intelligence is limited to the lower or concrete, earth-turned aspect of the mind. It is only man who begins to use for himself the other abstract, higher, or spiritual aspect of mind; and in the center of the whole is the all-important factor which differentiates

him from the animal and, as he develops, becomes his self-conscious individuality. The animal thus sits astride the fourth etheric level, its upper limit being the middle of the mental world. Man's range, however, runs only from the middle etheric, its upper limit being the middle atmic—itself astride the middle of the mental world, though as yet human consciousness functions largely on the animal side of the middle point.

Once the germ of individuality is implanted in him, not only is his potential range enlarged by extension into new realms beyond the level at which individuality appears, but also man, *as man*, withdraws his inner self from the dense physical level, and in shutting off its direct and open influence on him the fourth etheric level becomes his furthest or deepest point of descent into matter.

At the same time, he remains in very close touch with this dense world. This touch, however, is not by direct interchange of energy currents, but by a process exactly similar to that of electrical induction in a transformer, where there is no direct connection between primary and secondary circuits, but each influences the other because of the proximity between the two. The fourth ether acts like the core of the transformer, which at once separates and links the two circuits. Psychologically, the dense physical is now the real world to him: the place of objects which he soon begins to

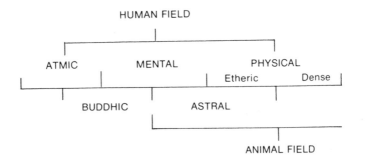

Diagram 2. To illustrate the overlap between human and animal fields

know are outside the subjective field of self. He reaches out into it in action, and influences it. It makes itselft felt inside him through sensation. But there is intrinsically a barrier—represented by the physical skin as well as by mental traits—between I-within and not-I-without.

This principle is simple enough. But in practice it is complicated and confused by the overlap of animal life of the physical body into the human sphere. For this animal life brings with it instinctive patterns, and hence emotional urges of a simple, primitive order, and conditions human intelligence towards satisfying these. Also, the human being, for a long time in his evolution, identifies himself with these instinctive urges, applying more than animal intellect towards satisfying them. Much of human behavior can, indeed, be analyzed into the primitive impulse to survive, to reproduce, to satisfy hunger, and so on. Hence the bridge mechanism, which both links and separates him from the dense physical, remains incomplete, both as a separator and transmitter of impulses between the two levels.

The human psyche thus has in it two main components. One is turned earthward, and is at times called "lunar", because it is said in occultism to be the aftermath of evolutionary developments on the earlier planetary chain of which our moon is the remnant. The other is the positive evolutionary one which should lead man's consciousness from earth to sun, and is thus called "solar". Both of these are reflected into the etheric field seen as a whole.

All this is said from the point of view of function. That is, it suggests the manner in which the middle etheric acts, and gives a key to many problems connected with health and disease, both physical and mental: semi-permeable because the animal aspects of the psycho-physical organism flow backward and forward through it, while solar, or spiritual-psychic consciousness stops short when it reaches it.

So far we have considered the fourth etheric level only in general terms, and as a reservoir of energy. But it has another special function in connection with the nervous system. This system, viewed from the physiological angle, is of a

quite special nature, the cells of which it consists having qualities absent in any other tissue. For many of these cells are enormously extended in one direction. The main body of the cell may be at one end of a filament several feet long, while even the largest of other cells are at most microscopic in size. Moreover, unlike any other tissue, a nerve cell never regenerates or duplicates itself. True, the *fiber* of the cell can regenerate, but never the cell itself. So we have a special case of organic tissue which is unlike any other in the body.

Similarly, at the etheric level, we have a special area of function in connection with the nervous system. As in all other organs and tissues, there is a complete duplicate of the physical structure in the etheric field: there are vital etheric brain and nervous systems, just as there are physical ones. The particular functions with which they are concerned are not only those of governing automatic, reflex action in the body, but also of linking the individual within to the dense world, thus making physical consciousness possible.

It is here that the fourth etheric link shows itself in its most significant form. For it acts as a screen on which (a) physical sense percepts register and are perceived by the indwelling mind; and also one in which (b) the contents of the mind itself are thrown, and through which they may become known to physical waking consciousness.

If, as in the case of a person drugged or unconscious from shock, illness, or deep hypnosis, the external impulses fail to penetrate the screen, the mind remains unaware of them: this layer is dislocated, or nonresponsive. In reverse direction, too, lack of sensitivity and response in this layer makes the individual act as an automaton, unaware of his own thoughts and feelings, without self-direction: in short, he acts much as an animal would. For, owing to the ambiguity of man, it is possible to dislocate the *human* elements of consciousness without unduly impairing the attributes of *animal* existence and vitality.

This level is consequently the main operative one in producing various forms of unconsciousness, both the natural one of sleep and the less normal ones of anesthesia, shock, or hypnosis.

Sleep, ideally, as in the case of young children or animals, is from the psychic angle associated with a release of tension in the denser triad of energy streams, those connected with the bodily framework. In waking consciousness, as we have indicated, the whole sevenfold etheric field acts as a coherent whole. This means that the levels corresponding to mental function work through the central fourth, putting thereby a certain strain on the bodily levels, which both isolates them from the circumambient general field of energies in the atmosphere and the earth, and makes them subservient to the direction of consciousness in the physical world. In sleep this stress is loosened, and in consequence in the barrier between the somatic field and the general currents in the etheric become re-connected with Nature, and this part of the system becomes recharged with its own kind of energies, in preparation for a new period of consciously directed activity during which these energies are consumed in work.

The success of this depends very much on the ability of the individual to let go of his body, and so allow it to sleep profoundly and relaxed. As is well-known, worry and mental stress are the main causes of insomnia or restlessness; for the mind, and its related energy streams in the subtler part of the etheric, are at least as active in sleep as when focused through the fourth into the physical brain. This activity is shown to us in some measure during the process of waking—of re-linking the physio-chemical field with the psychic—in the form of dreams, or other remembering.

Normal sleep is a state of poised suspense, and one in which the organs which transmit mental activity to the physical body, the chakras, are quiescent yet able to resume their activity at once when required.

Anesthesia, however, though the picture is similar to that of sleep, is due to disconnection between the chemical (somatic) and the psychic fields by the use of drugs: chemical substances having specific effect in paralyzing the fourth level, which is inhibited and made nontransmitting.

It is well-known that the drugs used act gradually and also that they can be selective. General anesthesia can be light or deep; some drugs dull pain while full mental awareness is

retained, and others act first on the mind and do not affect sense registration until large doses have been administered. Yet in all cases the point of action is the fourth level, which is not a simple mechanism, but a highly elaborate channel with many different functions represented in it.

Hypnosis is similar in its results, but here the agent is the mind, working on a type of etheric field in which the fourth level is unstable and easily inhibited. In other words, psychological dissociation occurs readily, because the psychospiritual and the physio-chemical fields are not properly integrated. There is still a great deal of vagueness in the individual as between himself and the natural world around him. His "lunar" aspects are in evidence, overlapping the fourth level, so that the latter is not under the proper control of the will, or "solar" aspect.

It makes little difference whether the hypnosis is self-induced or whether it is induced by another person. For in either case, it is caused by the impact of an *alter ego* on the fourth level, driving the two halves of the physical personality apart. This *alter ego*, in the case of a hypnotist working on a subject is, clearly, himself intruding on his victim's field—the source of influence he obtains over the latter. In the case of self-hypnosis, it is a complex in the subject's own mind, consisting of aspects of himself not recognized and consciously accepted by himself as *ego*. When the process of self-hypnosis is deliberately cultivated, as in developing mediumship, such a complex generally becomes personalized, and then called a guide.

Needless to say, the more often hypnosis is induced and the more often drugs are used to dim consciousness, the weaker the link between the two aspects of the etheric field becomes, the less definite the function of the "fourth".

Shock, producing temporary unconsciousness, whether total or only of pain, also represents a dislocation between the two sides of the field. This is accompanied by a sudden tightening of the aura and of the chakras, which are paralyzed. This is followed by relaxation into confusion and incoherence of the whole system, which only gradually returns to normal.

Emotional shock frequently produces enduring effects locally in the solar plexus center, which may remain tightly clamped, so that the sufferer "has no feeling about anything"; or alternatively it splays wide open so that everything becomes exaggerated and accompanied by over-reaction.

These principles appear simple enough: the ideal human being should have his fourth etheric diaphragm clear and steady. But in practice things are not ideal because man is far from having fulfilled himself, and is still in part animal.

Difficulty arises because man mentally identifies himself with the animal, and so with the physical world, and remains entangled in it. This is naturally correct enough for an animal, but in man it represents a backward-looking state rather than the teleological or solar one from which he has to learn to function as evolution proceeds. If he can learn to function in a solar manner—with positive self-direction and self-consciousness—this identification ceases. The result is that the fourth etheric level is then less a rather flaccid membrane than a clear glass-like screen between subjective and objective and perception. And, paradoxically, when this happens, objects in the physical world are more clearly perceived than before, because they are seen objectively and detachedly. Action in that world also has a more positive and dynamic quality, because the acting self is not influenced and dragged around by the things taking place in that world, but works outward directly, from a stable center. One may compare the detached individual to one standing on firm ground and observing things around him. The other is like a man afloat on the sea, on an unstable medium which carries him here and there on its currents, and tosses him on its waves. Clear observation under these circumstances is very difficult, and his point of observation is always uncertain.

Thus the middle etheric level is a most important link and barrier through which the individual makes contacts from within outward and from outside inward, between himself and the physical world. *All* physical consciousness depends on it, while the nature and quality of the consciousness depends on the integrity and stability of the fourth etheric film.

These, in turn, result from the state of mind and emotion of the individual within. If unconscious and automatic, physical consciousness will be repetitive and of the nature of reflex action. If steady and properly controlled by self-awareness, physical consciousness becomes clear, things are properly understood, and life will be governed by the indwelling self.

If, on the other hand, the person is—as most people are—in an intermediate stage, where animal and human elements are both active in the psyche, disharmony and conflict occur, and both clarity of physical consciousness and health are impaired. The middle layer of the etheric is then neither permeable as in the animal, nor crystal clear and stable as in the man who has achieved, but it is stretched and pulled like a piece of material under strain.

12

Psychological Implications

In the last chapter we have suggested that the middle point of
the etheric field is highly critical not only for health and
function at the physical level, but also for that of consciousness. It is from the viewpoint of the latter that we have now to
study the matter.

From the psychological angle two main points stand out.
First there is the oft-repeated fact that this level is that
through which all the phenomena concerned with waking
consciousness have to pass. Without it man would be entirely
cut off from conscious contact with the dense physical world.
He might be alive and aware of himself in other spheres, but
he would neither receive impulses from the dense physical,
nor would he be able in any way to influence it by action.

This may seem inconsistent with the fact that certain
levels of life continue when the individual is anesthetized or
otherwise rendered unconscious, or during normal sleep. Yet
if we remember that the field of animal (as distinct from
human) life overlaps this level, the difficulty is explained.
For it is higher functions of consciousness which are abro-
gated during these times, while the lower biological levels
continue to work until death finally separates the two halves
of the etheric field at that central point. One may even sur-
mise that, since animals can be anesthetized and made unconscious in much the same way as human beings, it is those
parts of the animal mentality which overlap with the human
which are affected and dislocated, while those below the
threshold of human life proper remain largely intact and
keep the unconscious body alive.

The second point is, once more, that while the entire
etheric field reflects the whole of the human being, including

the functions we call consciousness, the etheric itself has no consciousness of its own apart from the primitive elemental response belonging to the material of which it is made.* In this respect it is something like the nerves which carry impulses of pain or other sensation yet, if pressed on or damaged, indicate nothing of the fact that that damage is to themselves. That is, a sensory nerve may itself be anesthetic despite the fact that it conveys aesthetic or sensory impulses along its fibers.

It is important also to have a conception of the difference in principle between the animal and the man, with special reference to the fourth etheric level. For while the whole field, at all levels, is a picture of the inner individual, the focus of his conscious awareness and of his mind is to be sought at the physical level, in this fourth layer. In other words, the principle called in Sanskrit *Manas*, and meaning pure mind, or mind-as-such, impinges directly on this fourth level and from it conditions the rest of the field both upwards into the subtler levels and downward into the dense physical. Hence any alteration in the activity of *Manas* directly shows itself in alteration of the fourth etheric layer.

It is generally accepted by students of the occult that the difference between an animal and a man is due to an inner change call individualization. That is, man is no longer merged in a group soul, but has a soul of his own, in the center of which is the Monadic attribute of Will or Atma. Moreover, there are hints here and there in the literature, of the close relationship between this Atmic principle, that of Manas, and the physical etheric. And, while the *worlds* or planes where these principles reside correspond closely to one another, so do the human *principles* which belong to those worlds. The focal point of the latter is in the middle or fourth

---

*The word *consciousness* is best used in the sense given in the Oxford English Dictionary which equates it with the ability to know a thing as apart from oneself. Hence it implies the power to differentiate oneself from the object of which one is conscious. This is the beginning of the next phase, in which the observing "I" becomes aware of itself also as observer. The first certainly applies to animals, but more doubtfully to lower creatures. The second stage is essentially that of a fairly sophisticated human being.

level of each of these worlds. Thus the process of individualization can be envisaged as being due to the linking up of the animal mind with the source of Monadic power, Atma. As a result, when the process is fully accomplished, there is in man a very different state of affairs at these levels from that which exists in the animal. Atma, making itself felt in Manas, glavanizes it into a full activity which entirely alters the field of the mind as a whole; and this activity changes the quality of the fourth etheric so that it reflects a consciousness which is at once entirely detached from any identification either with objects in the physical world or states within the mind, and which is nevertheless entirely aware of the whole of these.

This is, of course, an ideal and an ultimate state. It takes little observation to realize that in man's present stage the group soul habit persists, sometimes obviously, as in that form of automatic patriotism and loyalty where these are not thought out and deliberately accepted. Sometimes the tendency is less patent, as in the many subtle and insidious ways in which a person lets himself be affected by others without in the least knowing that he is doing so.

In other words, individualization, while it represents a step *doubtless* irreversible, does not mean that the individual has done more than begin on the path which will eventually lead him to full individuality. He is still largely at the mercy of his animal ancestry and evolutionary pattern and, indeed, the whole struggle of his existence is teleological, towards achieving and making actual the individuality which is latent within him. To do this means altering his animal nature, without doing it violence, so that it becomes part of the pattern of life and consciousness of the spiritualized man.

This digression into psychology from a spiritual angle is not irrelevant to the subject of the etheric field. For it shows that, at the central level, there have to be forces which are ever trying to close the open field which is proper to the animal. Yet they must not obscure the clarity of vision which that field needs if it is to be a true reflection of the "stone of pure die or perfect cube" which is the mind, and against

which all percepts and concepts can be tried for truth and accuracy.

In practice, therefore, we have here a mixed activity as between the automatic, reflex-like reactions of the animal mind, and the controlled, chosen and aware actions of the truly human mentality. From a more technical angle, one may say that one has here a mixture between the forces of the collective *sub*conscious and the *super*conscious. The former is the garnered collective experience of animals and lower biological kingdoms—instinct. The latter, the *super*-conscious, represents those aspects of consciousness which are also collective in the sense that they are uni-versal—as Jung and others point out in their discussion of myth and religious symbols—but which have not yet passed through the field of explicit experience. This they must even-tually do for each individual man. In the middle of these opposite pulls is the mind of man; and the center of the physical incarnation of that mind is the fourth etheric level.

Passing on from this, we can consider the role of the etheric field in ordinary life and one's awareness of it in the waking state. One sees man's mind focused at a critical point between the real world—that of dense physical objects which retain their shape, size and relationships independently of himself, and the subjective world within the mind. The first is a world of what has been called "absolute space and time", and where these depend primarily on themselves and not on the mind of the percipient. They would still be there if the mind were not observing them. The second, however, is a place where space and time are apparently fluid and plastic so that the contrast between what happens in the mind and the fixity of the dense physical world makes us think of our dreams and our visions as fantastic and unreal. This is due to their inconsequence, and the ability of things to change instantly into new forms, or of time to seem to pass with more than lightning rapidity. The mind (which is heavily conditioned to working con-sciously in terms of physical space-time) cannot but be dis-concerted by the waywardness of mental activity; while the kind of person whose mind is predominantly active and ab-

stract finds the drag of trying to express his thoughts in material form and a great weariness.

There thus seems to be a radical difference between the realms on either side of the etheric screen. So the question arises as to the form in which, on the one hand, perception of the physical world reaches the indwelling mind and, on the other, of the form in which mental events such as dreams exist in and around that mind before becoming expressed in the familiar language of physical objects and people. In other words, do the pictures imprinted on the sensory mechanism, and ultimately recognized as physical events, travel through the screen and into the mind in the same way as a lantern slide is projected along the ray of light which carries it on to the sheet on which it becomes visible? And would such a thing as a mental image or a dream, if seen in the mental world itself, exist in the same explicit and pictorial form as that in which we see it in waking consciousness? The answer is almost certainly not; the pictorial form depends on the connection of the mind with the etheric screen and, where human cognition is concerned, with *Manas* at the fourth etheric level.

What then seems to happen when we perceive a physical object? It is well-known that the light image imprinted on the retina is not transmitted to the brain except in the form of nerve impulses. The same applies to sound striking the ear. It is only in the brain that these dots and dashes travelling along certain nerves become integrated into an image or a meaningful sound which, in the case of an animal says "food" or "danger" or "mate" and so calls forth the appropriate instinctive reaction. In man, where *Manas* is an active principle, this integrative process is carried further, so that he can say, "This is an apple" or "The edge of a cliff" or "Jane Smith", identifying the thing perceived irrespective of whatever action he takes either automatically or after due judgment.

It is reasonable to think that the same chain of events occurs if, instead of considering the sense organ and the nerve and the cerebral cortex, we think of the etheric screen, the

field of the mind (*kama-manas*) and *Manas* itself. A certain series of stimuli throw an image onto the etheric screen from the outer, or dense, physical side. Passing through it, they become relayed to *Manas* through a field conditioned by past experience. Therefore it drags with it associations derived from that experience. *Manas* then becomes aware of the stimuli reaching it, and the perceptive act is accomplished. But it is not an image so much as energy waves which exist on the inner side of the etheric screen.

This process is akin to that used in radar. For there the apparatus radiates certain waves of energy into the atmosphere. When these encounter objects they return to the receiving apparatus, creating on it certain changes which are related to the object from which they come. But they are not in a form in which they can be recognized as such until they have been transformed within the apparatus and thrown onto the screen as light and shadow patterns. Then, only, are they known for what they are.

The objection may now be raised that the mind is not a radar transmitter and does not send waves out from itself. But indeed this is not so. For if the mind did not project something of itself outward through the etheric field there would be no relation between it and the physical world. It is this projection which is the so-called astro-mental body. The term *body* is perhaps a little misleading, though it can be called one of the vestures of the spiritual man, it is better thought of as a field of energy rather than as a solid object, just as the etheric field exists as such only by virtue of its interweaving streams of energy.

We may suppose further that the ovoid form described for this body by clairvoyants is due to the place from which it is observed. For careful thought will suggest to us that the principle called *Manas* is nondimensional: it is a point which has no size, despite its importance as the center of the whole personal field. If, then, from this point energy is radiated toward the three-dimensional etheric, it would, if observed from the etheric end, appear to have dimensional extension

and a more or less measurable size. Seen in this way it is evident that the ovoid aura enclosing the etheric aura proper derives its form and size from its contact with that aura, and that if one were able to move upward or inwared to that mental realm itself apart from any etheric connection, the form would tend to become less and less evident.

What then would be left? A further analogy suggests itself. It, too, comes from radar. For the mental field would probably be something like the region between the receiving aerial and the screen: a series of energy waves of varying intensity, and not a place of formed images.

Perhaps this concept can be made plainer by another analogy. This time, however, it shows the process in reverse: where the mind, having become active, projects that action outwards toward physical consciousness. In television, the essential factor is the tube, with a narrow end containing electrodes. Then comes a space which is, when active, filled with streams of energy (cathode rays) of rapidly varying intensity. When these streams strike the flourescent screen at the broad (viewing) end, what was hitherto dark becomes a light image of a kind intelligble to the physical eye and to our knowledge of physical things. Until then, however, there is no formed image. The electrodes represent *Manas*, the space in the tube equates with the mind or astro-mental body and the screen with the etheric.

One may therefore suppose that were we able to observe what we eventually know as a dream, *at its own level*—in the psychic, astro-mental field, before it made itself known to the waking man—it would be formless as the waves in the television tube are formless. (This word "formless" must be taken here only as referring to physical forms extended in space and time.) But when we wake up and remember our dream it has become projected onto the etheric screen and there has acquired the kind of objective structure which we know so well. It retains some of its intrinsic mental characters in its fluidity and plasticity.

We may now ask ourselves what determines the forms of presentation of a dream. That is probably derived from the

animal aspects of the mind, and of memory—the collective of Jung in the aspect we have suggested should be called *sub*conscious. That is, not only do we use our memories of everyday things, in the way Freud has described—if not for the purpose he suggests—as well as drawing on the deeper, racial memories for the more mythological images which form so important a part of Jung's psychology. In other words, the *human* mind meets the *animal* mind at this point in order to acquire a language in which to express its own intrinsic activity in a form intelligible to the waking man. The images, in short, are symbolic representations of psychic and spiritual activity, their nature being derived from the collective past of the race.

We can carry our study somewhat further by still using the television tube analogy, as this will give us an idea of the difference between sleeping and waking consciousness. For it appears as if, when we are awake, the focus of *Manas* which we call "I", the observer and actor, is projected through the etheric screen into close touch with the dense physical world. It is then in the position of the television viewer, able to watch from outside the apparatus what is being shown on the screen and to take an intelligent interest in it. In sleep, however, it is as if the point of self-identity were withdrawn behind the screen into the tube, where "I" now find myself, did not quite reach the screen so that no image is thrown on it and the body can rest properly. "I" would then find itself, for the most part, inward turned and unable to see explicit images. Hence it is only when I wake up that I can be effective and intelligent both about myself and about things around me. To be equally effective and positively active during sleep would require a degree of self-awareness and consciousness in the mental world comparable to that we have when awake in the physical world.

At the same time, such full comprehension can only be achieved as the etheric screen becomes clarified and undistorting. Or, perhaps more exactly, when nothing intervenes between it and *Manas*. For most people it is as if one's windowpane were colored and warped, from outside by physical

impurities in food, hygiene, etc.; from inside by thoughts and feelings based on animal instinctive needs, however much they may have been modified by the human mind. And in both cases the distorting factor is where the subhuman, animal remnants affect what should ultimately be an aspect of man controlled and directed solely by himself through his manasic principle in its pure, unconditioned form.

In this way we see that the relation between the inner and the outer, physical man, both psychic and spiritual, depends on the etheric field and especially on the focus of *Manas* at the fourth or central level. Moreover, it seems that this inner man can only be properly comprehended when observed from outside the screen, in full waking consciousness: whence no doubt the insistence in all schools of spiritual teaching on the importance of physical life in order to perfect and fulfil any spiritual realization one may have.

At the same time, such full comprehension can only be achieved as the etheric screen becomes clarified and undistorting. Or, perhaps more exactly, when nothing intervenes between it and *Manas*. For most people it is as if one's windowpane were colored and warped, from outside by physical impurities in food, hygiene, etc.; from inside by thoughts and feelings based on animal instinctive needs, however much they may have been modified by the human mind. And in both cases the distorting factor is where the subhuman, animal remnants affect what should ultimately be an aspect of man controlled and directed solely by himself through his manasic principle in its pure, unconditioned form.

13

Psychic Phenomena

This chapter is intended to touch only on certain limited aspects of psychic phenomena. A fuller analysis of actual events and possible explanations is to be found in our book, *This World and That* (published by Faber & Faber), and need not be repeated here.

What concerns us now is the function of the etheric field in the production of phenomena, whether these be perceptive or psychokinetic—in spiritualistic language, *physical*. For just as all psychological phenomena have to pass through the etheric field—and its fourth level in particular—to reach physical consciousness, so must all parapsychological events.

Before we consider this, however, it may be well to state what appears to be a basic fact: that such things as telepathy (and probably other modes of extrasensory perception) are fairly certainly a common and constant occurrence at the mental level. But it is the exception rather than the rule that they penetrate the barrier of the etheric field and so make themselves known to physical waking consciousness. This is in part due to unresponsiveness in the fourth etheric level, but it is also due to the fact that we are so busily occupied with physical action, and with the enormous crowd of physical impressions which are constantly assailing our senses. We therefore pay little attention to the subtler and, usually, rather muted stream of extrasensory impacts which underlie them.

That this is so, is not so strange as might appear. Many years ago Wilfred Trotter suggested in his book, *The Herd Instinct*, that social behavior was due to some sort of mental intercommunication behind the scenes; while the concept of the collective unconscious also allows for similar mind-to-

mind activity. What is now said is the same thing, in different and more mechanistic terms. The principle is not difficult to accept on the perceptive side. On the kinetic side it is a little more complicated, because genuine physical phenomena in the seance room are now rare, whatever they may have been in the past, and require special conditions.

Here a further basic principle can be put forward: there are two orders of extrasensory perceptivity, one which is controlled by the will acting on the mind, and one which is not so controlled, but which is often unconscious, and so, apt to be erratic and uncertain when it does reach consciousness. The first is psychic capacity, associated with the conscious, it is controlled by the mind and reaches physical consciousness by means of the etheric brain, and particularly the chakras in the head. The second is of a more primitive order and is a potent factor in the ordering of instinctive life. Its main impact is through the solar plexus chakra, and the sympathetic nervous system. In practice, while the first is essentially human and solar, the second is animal or lunar. But in common with the rest of human life, most human beings are at a stage where elements of both levels are active.

There is a great deal of difference between the two. For one depends on the ability of the etheric to reflect or transmit a clear, focused image, while the other relies on more passive permeability, or the direct flow of impulses through the fourth level. The mental percipient chooses and focuses on the matter in hand. The more primitive has to take what comes indiscriminately, and without being able to select or concentrate on any part of it. The first is a faculty which can be used by the one who possesses it for careful scientific research. The second may produce interesting information, but this is likely to be of more use to the ouside observer than it is to the person through which it comes—as, for instance, the sitter rather than to the medium in a spiritualistic seance.

Once more, these generalizations deal with principles, and in practice most psychic people are not pure types of either order. Further, it is possible for such a person deliberately to

train himself to function more on one side than the other. The one who sets to work intelligently to study his psychic perceptivity in full awareness and with no diminution of physical consciousness, will gradually make his etheric screen taut and clear. The one who passively "sits for development", on the other hand, is deliberately loosening the fabric of his etheric and putting it back once again to the state it was in during early life and the more primitive phases of human development. But apart also from negative practices, the cultivation of psychic perceptivity as an end in itself, through hypnosis, self-induced or otherwise, by means of drugs, or by such things as concentrating on a chakra, will also develop a form of psychism which can only be confusing and unintegrated with the conscious mind. For it is only when the head centers are properly activated from above that clear understanding can be achieved—and that as much in the psychological as in the psychic sphere.

For it must be realized that, just as fine discrimination is required in order to understand the physical world, so is it required for perceiving the nonphysical. This is all the more important because of the fluidity and lack of sharp barriers in the psychic realm. As a result, it is very easy—and, in fact, it is almost the rule, in many instances—for a percipient to confuse the images produced in his own mind with those of psychic objects and situations not so produced, but existing in their own right outside himself. Such discrimination depends not only on clear thinking, but also on thinking directed by the will. And, as we have already suggested, the will can be brought to bear not only on the mind itself, and mainly through this on to the etheric organism, it has also a direct control of this organism particularly on and through its fourth level.

It follows from this that if the perceptive function is intelligently and deliberately directed, the etheric field will, apart from disturbances such as arise from physical ill-health, etc., be smooth and clear. In it and through it the individual will then perceive clearly and with fine focus. But if there is turmoil and stress all percepts become distorted, while the

deliberate removal of control in states of trance, hypnosis or drugs will allow it to be swayed and ruffled by every psychic breeze which touches it.

Physical phenomena in principle can be associated with either type of psychic perceptivity. That is, a person with full control of his faculties, and who has learned how, can perform acts of magic at the dense physical level. Primitive magic and sorcery need to be included in this class of occurrence. But such people are extremely rare in the West, while in the East [and in Africa] such acts are usually done by fakirs and people of that order, who perhaps spend years in learning to do what amounts to a single psychokinetic conjuring trick. In any case the spiritually integrated person will not show off or demonstrate his capacities in this direction except for some extremely good reason.

Most commonly, in the West, physical phenomena are associated with mediums, and take place either in the seance room or in the form of poltergeist occurrences. It is as well to say at once that genuine phenomena are increasingly rare, whereas doubtful and spurious ones are common. *

In any case, all genuine phenomena, whether concerning the fall of dice (as in experimental work), materializations, apports or raps, depend on what is called psychokinetic (PK) factor in the mind. Certain general conditions govern their occurrence.

1. *Mental direction.* All physical phenomena are in some way purposive, even if that purpose is not immediately apparent. In laboratory experiments with dice mechanically dropped, the purpose is to throw more sixes or ones, or combinations of six and one (or any other such target number) than chance will allow. In poltergeist phenomena the purpose may be obscure, the mind directing them being perhaps the unconscious side of the focal agent's own mind, maybe another

---

*It is noted here that this book was originally written in 1957 which was considerably before the advent of such thoroughly tested persons as Uri Geller, Olga Kulagina of the U.S.S.R., Matthew Manning of England and the many English and Japanese school children who are demonstrating under strict laboratory conditions such psychokinetic actions as bending steel, silverware, and disrupting well protected scientific equipment. Editor

influencing the agent. In materialization during a seance the mental agent may be the medium, the sitters, or the mind of another person, alive or dead.

2. *Energy.* When a physical object is moved, sound produced, or a form materialized, work (in the scientific sense) is done, and hence, a source of energy is required. It is here that the etheric field is involved, the energy being drawn from that. In seances, with a circle of people, the medium is the prime mover, but energy appears also to be drawn from the sitters; which is why they so often feel cold or exhausted after the seance is over. In poltergeist phenomena, too, there is always some mediumistic person—often a rather unbalanced adolescent, or a simple adult—who is the focus around which the phenomena occur. The presence nearby of vigorous animal life, such as horses or cows in a stable, is also known to make them stronger, as if energy were drawn from them and used by the directing mind.

These rules apply to all forms of phenomena, whether they consist of raps, table turning or anything else. And though no visible rods or levers are seen, they must fall into the same category as where visible manifestation takes place, and the mysterious substance known as *ectoplasm* is formed and seen. The latter appears basically to be no different from the immediate and invisible cause of apports or movement of furniture except in its density. Indeed, though not visible to the human eye, a photographic plate will sometimes show slightly materialized forms known as "extras", which suggest that there are many kinds and degrees of ectoplasm long before the visible, tangible stage is reached. Hence the generalizations about its mechanism which follow:

1. Physical phenomena never seem to occur around people with crisp integrated personalities. The presence of such people may, in fact, inhibit their occurrence.

2. The focus of origin is always where there is an etheric field which is loose, permeable and unstable.

3. Nothing has ever been written which indicates the exact mode of formation of ectoplasm. Careful observaton over a long period seems to suggest that the operative level of the

phenomena is at the fourth and denser levels of the etheric field. But this can only be accomplished when the materializing medium has made himself psychologically passive and inert: psychologically speaking, genuine dissociation has to occur. This is complete, if only temporary, abdication of control over himself. In this way the higher etheric levels are inactive, and the lower levels can be manipulated in such a way that phenomena can take place.

It appears as if the directing mind were able, as it were, to dip through the fourth etheric level into the denser levels of the chemical ethers, and to draw energy material from them into the fourth level. At this level it is in an unstable state—comparable to the unstable condition of the single physical chemical atom (which belongs here) in its nascent phase. At this point, the operative mind appears to be able to push the material out of the field in its unstable form; and once outside it (in practice outside the ribbon round the dense body of the medium), it automatically tends to drop back to its proper level. That is, it densifies *toward* the solid level, taking on whatever form the purposive mind wishes. When the phenomena are over, the material automatically travels back into the medium's body by a reverse process. For there is a strong magnetic pull between the medium's etheric field and the extruded material which belongs to it. It has been possible to draw it out in this way only because of the plasticity of the etheric field of the medium.

The consistency of the material is very variable. As crude material it seems to be at its densest like rubbery foam—a soft solid. Cases are recorded in old literature where it flowed into a bowl like a liquid—though in one case at least when the hand was dipped into it, it did not wet the skin, showing that it did not readily separate into discrete parts, but tended to hold together: which would confirm the principle that it was magnetically tied to the medium. Most often it appears in a gaseous form, like thick fog, while in other cases nothing is visible to ordinary sight, yet something is formed which is capable of moving solid objects or of being photographed. The latter, seen clairvoyantly, looks like rods an inch or so across,

of a darkish blue-grey color, almost indigo, against the pearly grey luminosity which is the general etheric background at this level, even in physical darkness. These rods are sometimes able to stand dim red and infrared light, but they tend to disperse and break up at once if any brighter light is allowed into the room.

It is because of the intimate link between the medium and his own extruded etheric that any sudden break-up of materialized ectoplasm is such a serious shock to him. It is as if stretched elastic snapped violently back into the very middle of a delicate organism.

Poltergiest phenomena obviously do not fulfill all these conditions, if only because they often take place in broad daylight. They are, however, rare and have such a way of not happening in the presence of people who are alert and observant that it has not been possible to study them directly. But it seems as if the general principle holds good, that they are purposive. But the purpose seems to be more due to blind emotion than to thought. Sometimes, in fact, it would appear as if the directing agent was simply a mischievous imp rather than even a primitive human mind—which may very well be literally the case.

In discussing ectoplasm we have been concerned with a process of making subtle energy matter dense—bringing it nearer to the solid state. But it sometimes happens that solid objects are apparently carried from afar through walls and closed doors, appearing in the seance room in their original state. Such genuine apports are rare, and no direct study of the phenomena has been possible, but there is considerable evidence that they can take place. In the light of the principles we have been discussing there is no theoretical reason why it should not be possible temporarily to disperse matter, making it etheric, and so able to pass through solid objects such as walls, and then allow it to return to its original form once inside the seance room. In other words, a process takes place of ectoplastic formation in reverse, the matter of the object brought being magnetically held together in the form of that object, so that when the dispersing forces are removed

it recrystallized into its original form. This appears a probable explanation—although it must be fully admitted to theoretical and not based on direct experience.

14

Group Work and Ceremonial

Group and herd phenomena have long been a matter of interest to students of psychology and sociology. For it is evident that there are occasions when members of a crowd or an audience remain cold and discrete, while at other times, perhaps unexpectedly, and on a sudden impulse, a number of people, even a whole nation coalesce into a collective entity capable of anything from the most sublime to the most bestial actions.

Looked at from the point of view of the etheric field, the difference between single people and a group depends upon whether or not a common aura exists. A crowd of people walking down a street consists of separate individuals, each within his own auric field. But it must be remembered that, behind the etheric levels proper, there is the mind, which is only partly personal and separate. There is, besides the personal mind, a collective mental level, where the individual is merged into a general field of thought and feeling.

Two factors facilitate this. One is physical proximity, especially in a room or building. Thus it is difficult for people living in a crowded house, even among strangers, to remain immune and aloof from the atmosphere of the place as a whole. Even in open country, if the attention of a number of people becomes drawn to some object or event, there is a tendency for a group aura to form, so long as the situation holds its interest. Thus a concert or theatrical perfomance provides both factors—physical proximity in an enclosed space, and a focus of interest—so that a group atmosphere soon develops. But, equally, an accident or a common danger, in street or country, may draw ordinary people together into a group which may be a panic-stricken mob, a riotous or hostile crowd, or one which is emotionally carried away by a

popular evangelist, a political speaker, or a piece of national pagenantry.

The nature and quality of such a group will depend not only on the common temperamental traits of those involved, but also on the object which draws them together. It can thus be on a level of deep devotion or esthetic appreciation, or it can be a mob whose main passion is fear or destructive hysteria. In any case, a holistic phenomenon takes place, and the power of the group, in whatever direction it runs, is greater than the sum of that of the individuals of which it consists. That is, there is a *plus* quantity in the group aura, which is derived from the level of devic-elemental life and which corresponds to the quality of the thought and feeling of the group, and immediately reinforces the human contribution. It seems as if this factor, which is always and at all times operative within the individual, becomes multiplied in a geometrical rather than an arithmetical proportion when the etheric entity is no longer a single human being but a collective group.

A number of other factors besides common interest also come into play. Thus, where there is a leader, he is an important king-pin of the group aura. He may be a lecturer, an actor, a priest, the chairman of a company, a governor, or the ruler of a country: in any case, he is a focus capable up to a point of both holding and breaking up a group aura, and also of giving it a certain coloring. This is especially strong if the leader is thrown up as an embodiment of some collective mental movement in a nation, or if he fulfils an archetypal role such as that of a king or high priest. If, in addition, ritual forms are used—especially ancient ones, hallowed by tradition—or if, as in Catholic churches, there is a consecrated physical object as a focus, the group aura tends to be more consistent and stronger than it would otherwise be.

At a concert of good music the general aura becomes filled with a fine quality of feeling, and a strong degree of whatever intuitive coloring corresponds to the music, the devic aspect being in harmony with it. In India there is a tradition about the *gandharvas*, or music devas, while in the West the

cherubim have always been associated with angelic choirs. At a concert of the more lurid and raucous forms of rock music the devic aspects will be a more earthy elemental order, tending to stimulate the more sensual aspects of people. In a group endeavoring to study the deeper meaning of life the aura will be correspondingly different, while that of a popular evangelical meeting will possibly be strongly emotional, and can run over into hysteria.

Where a national event such as a coronation is involved, the whole country—and, indeed, the whole Commonwealth—acquires a vast common aura, the separate parts of it becoming closely knit. For here we have a potent combination of factors, each bringing its own focus to bear on the sovereign who is the central pivot of the united group. There is the general emotional appeal to the subjects of the nation, the action which is to bring the majority into tune with one another. There is the outward pageantry, ancient and traditional, reinforcing the first. And, further, there is the movement in the deeper, collective aspects of every individual, which is projected outward to the one who embodies the powerful archetypal symbol of the sovereign: an *avatar* or incarnation of the spiritual ruler, the will, in every man. In addition to all this there is added the potency of the sacramental aspect of the ritual of coronation, which, in itself, directly invokes forces from the angelic kingdoms. All these things together weld the aura of a large group into a vast and, for the time being, united field of thought and feeling of loyalty, love, and patriotism, even if tinged with pure excitement and pleasure-seeking.

Looked at clairvoyantly, a group aura appears as a moving, pulsating globe of etheric material which envelops all those present. Through it the impulses of thought and feeling ripple like wind over a field of corn. The coloring will vary with the mood of the moment, and while at times the whole structure is comparatively quiescent, it may appear turbulent, as if tossed by a storm. Individuals who remain objective and ouside the collective impulse—a critic at a theater, a person wrapped up in his own thoughts during a lecture—are

perhaps geographically in the group aura, but do not become a part of it. Such people are like rocks in a stream of water—and may, indeed, sometimes cause eddies and cross currents in the group atmosphere, and in the actual auric structure in which the group thought and feeling are reflected.

An immense thing like the Commonwealth at a coronation cannot, clearly, have a single worldwide aura. Each nation or group of colonies will naturally tend to create its own, but on such an occasion there will be a close magnetic tie or link between each part. The response will possess a basic and univeral quality, but each spacially separated unit will supply a different overtone due to local variations in race, culture, etc., and thus produce its own active etheric field.

If the group principle is understood, some very practical considerations emerge, which concern leaders of classes for study or meditation. For it does not require a great deal of sensitivity to become aware of the formation of a group aura, and, equally, of its dispersal.

For one thing, no grouping can take place where argument rather than discussion is going on. Argument creates strain and tension, and is generally disruptive in quality, while discussion is another thing, and no matter how many different points of view arise, true discussion builds a structure and does not destroy it. If people, even of very different temperament and viewpoint, come together not merely to *hear* but to *listen* to one another, to try and find common ground and to seek out what is true in whatever is said, much good can come of it. For then a group aura forms, and the *plus* element can be so strong that not only are personal differences resolved, but a higher octave of understanding and insight into a difficult subject can be reached.

If however, a destructive comment is thrown in, or somebody breaks out of the common atmosphere in a burst of resentment or fear, the aura is apt to be irretrievably shattered. Similarly, fatigue inevitably comes after a time, and the whole structure falls slack and flags. A good leader may—with the cooperation of others—be able to steady an

emotionally-disturbed group, so that it picks up its tone again. But an hour's valuable and constructive study is often spoiled by being made to go on too long. Therefore a leader needs to be sensitive and watch for any change in the vitality of the group. For if fatigue has set in the light has gone, and whatever good has been touched may become lost in the mists of confusion, due to the fact that each etheric brain has carried all it can for the time being.

Postscript

In the foregoing chapters we have put forward, without equivocation, the thesis that man incarnate depends entirely on his vital etheric field for contact with the world of incarnation, the dense physical. And incarnation is, if we are to accept universal religious belief, for the purpose of spiritual regeneration and self-realization. Only so can the human being ever become the god-like being he has the ability to be. Without descending into matter he would remain a germ, impotent and sterile. Hence the importance of this etheric field in all phases of physical life, and not least in the development of the spiritual nature.

That a study of this vital field is no simple matter is evident both from what has been said and from what has obviously been left unsaid. We are very conscious that only the surface of the subject has been skimmed. At almost every point it would be possible to start a new train of investigation, branching out from the main theme in all kinds of directions.

One of these is the relationship between the intelligent life forces we call the devic kingdom, and man: an immense and fascinating subject which cannot be developed here. Without it a vast blank is left in the whole biological field. Yet, if there is any truth in the little we have said, it is evident that the biologist who seeks to create life—organisms which, however simple, have the capacity to reproduce, to mutate, etc.—in a test tube is following a forlorn hope. It would be only if he were able to enlist the help of the devic kingdom that he could supply the elusive *plus* which makes all the difference between a chemical molecule, however complex, and live matter such as a virus or a gene.

The same applies to the neuropsychologist, whose ap-

proach to life is from the cybernetic angle. A simple machine, with components made to represent the action of only two or three nerve cells is capable of behavior comparable to that of an animal. Hence, he argues, the interaction of scores of millions of such cells is the key to all the complexities of human behavior. But one thing will certainly never be reproduced by the machine, however far the cybernetic process is carried, and that is individual consciousness. It may produce robots able to do much of the automatic work now done by human beings, but robots they will remain. For consciousness is a thing which germinates in the higher animals and develops increasingly only in man. And, just as the biologist stops short of creating living matter, so the materialistic psychologist will inevitably fail to create individual consciousness, for the reason that the source of it is not in any machine.

To the physician the vital mechanism is obviously important. In fact, common phrases like *vitality, nervous energy,* and the like, indicate a more or less blind sense of it.

The depth psychologist goes further into the realm of human individuality and consciousness than does the academic. Some understanding of the vital field and the screen on to which waking consciousness is thrown both simplifies and makes objective many of the obscurities and complexities which arise when these things are thought of only in abstract and metaphysical terms. It shows, moreover, that what is seen in terms of waking consciousness is an epiphenomenon of the deeper psycho-spiritual life: an image cast by that life, but not the life itself. The dream symbol, therefore, no matter how much endowed with potency, is then realized as only the outermost garment of the indwelling reality, not the reality itself.

So one could multiply the implications to the scientist of the structural and functional ideas here outlined. That they are not to be taken as authoritative, dogmatic, or conclusive, is obvious. But if they serve as food for reflection and as a starting point for further research, that is as much as can be hoped.

To the student of the occult, also, the matter is important. For he, endeavoring to work from inside himself, in a realm which he often feels is beyond and superior to that of even the most spiritually-minded psychologist, is nevertheless an incarnate being. Physical health is vital to his work lest he break down both physically and mentally under stresses not properly understood and aligned to the needs of life in a fleshly body. But, more than this, it is only as he finds the poised, quiet center of the mind while he is awake and fully conscious, that he achieves anything worth while. The silent chatter which is the principal activity of the minds of most of us can be observed and controlled by the act of watching its activity on the etheric screen. It is only when this is constantly done and eventually achieved as a permanent state, that we shall lose the confusion of images and thoughts which are always before us, and which cause the semi-somnolence in which we pass most of our days: a somnolence in which we live half in a subjective dream state, and half in blurred awareness of the material world around us. If that mental poise, centered in the focus of unconditioned mind can be obtained, and all the clouds of association and memory be eliminated, so that it comes into direct relation with the etheric screen, waking life becomes a real thing, with full apprehension of both the without and the within. The range of human consciousness is then complete, from the spiritual to the material, through the mind.

So to think of the physical body as something more than an assembly of chemical molecules is, basically, to focus also on the spiritual man. For the above and the below are basically one, and to understand the one is to know also the other. The physical world is the spiritual expressed in explicit language. The spiritual is, by its very nature, implicit and abstract unless expressed through the mind in language we can understand. Hence the value of such a study as this, provided it is extended far enough to become illumined by the spiritual intuition, and to become effective through the human mind.

We publish books on:
Healing and Health ● Metaphysics and
Mysticism ● Transpersonal Psychology
Philosophy ● Religion ● Reincarnation,
Science ● Yoga and Meditation.
Other books of possible interest include:

At the Feet of the Master by *"Alcyone"*
Krishnamurti's precepts for right living

Beyond Individualism by *Dane Rudhyar*
From ego-centeredness to higher consciousness

Cayce, Karma and Reincarnation by *I. C. Sharma*
Similarity between philosophies of Cayce and India

The Choicemaker by *E. Howes & S. Moon*
Our need to make choices as vital to our evolution

Commentaries on Living by *J. Krishnamurti*
Series 1, 2 & 3. Dialogue on many aspects of living

A Great Awakening by *Robert Powell*
Comparison of Krishnamurti and Zen philosophies

Opening of the Wisdom Eye by *Dalai Lama*
The path of enlightenment through Buddhism

A Way to Self Discovery by *I. K. Taimni*
Way of life for serious aspirants of esoteric wisdom

Whispers from the Other Shore by *Ravi Ravindra*
How religion helps us search for the center of being

Wisdom, Bliss & Common Sense by *Darshani Deane*
Distills arcane secrets of self-transformation

Available from:
The Theosophical Publishing House
P. O. Box 270, Wheaton, Illinois 60189-0270